Freeway

Soziales

Englisch für berufliche Schulen

Vocabulary Notebook

von
Sabina Piatzer

Ernst Klett Verlag
Stuttgart · Leipzig

Freeway Soziales

Englisch für berufliche Schulen

Vocabulary Notebook

von Sabina Piatzer

Werkübersicht:
Schülerbuch, 978-3-12-800037-4
Lehrerhandbuch mit Lehrer-Service-DVD-ROM und 2 Audio-CDs, 978-3-12-800038-1
Workbook mit 1 Audio-CD, 978-3-12-800039-8
Vokabellernheft 978-3-12-800047-3
Schülerpaket: Workbook und Vokabellernheft, 978-3-12-800052-7
Freeway Online-Ergänzungen unter www.klett.de/online

1. Auflage 1 5 4 3 2 | 15 14 13 12 11

Projektleitung: Matthias Rupp
Redaktion: Redaktionsbüro Sabina Piatzer, Hannover
Herstellung: Angelika Lindner

Umschlaggestaltung: ya:design, Roman Triebelhorn, Stuttgart
Bildquellennachweis: COVER Avenue Images GmbH (Pixtal), Hamburg; Avenue Images GmbH (Maskot), Hamburg
Satz: Redaktionsbüro Sabina Piatzer, Hannover
Reproduktion: Ernst Klett Verlag GmbH, Stuttgart
Druck: Medienhaus Plump GmbH, Rheinbreitbach

Printed in Germany
ISBN 978-3-12-800047-3

9 783128 000473

Inhalt

Vocabulary and exercises

Abkürzungen und Symbole

BE	britisches Englisch
AE	amerikanisches Englisch
e.g.	Anwendungsbeispiel
=	synonym
↔	opposite
→	word family
·	Wörter aus anderen Units des Lehrbuchs

Service im Internet

Unter den **Freeway Online-Links** finden Sie die Vokabeln des Vocabulary Notebook zum Download im MP3-Format. Gehen Sie einfach auf www.klett.de und geben Sie den Online-Link in das Suchfeld ein. Weitere Hinweise erhalten Sie auf Seite 104.

Vorwort

Vokabeln sind das Einmaleins der Sprache. Sie sind unbedingt notwendig, um Texte zu verstehen, Fragen zu beantworten, Essays zu schreiben, Übersetzungen anzufertigen und vor allem natürlich, um korrekt zu sprechen.

Dieses Heft bietet Ihnen die Möglichkeit, Wortschatz aus Ihrem Lehrwerk zu festigen und zu erweitern, um sich effizient auf Ihre Fachhochschulreife-Prüfung vorbereiten zu können.

Wissenschaftliche Forschungen haben gezeigt, dass man sich thematisch sortierten Wortschatz besser einprägen kann als einfache Vokabellisten. Zu den so genannten Mnemotechniken zählt das Strukturieren von Vokabular in Wortfeldern. Darunter versteht man Zusammenstellungen von Wörtern, Strukturen und Redewendungen unter einem bestimmten Oberbegriff. In Unit 1 finden Sie zum Beispiel Vokabular aus *Freeway* zu den Oberbegriffen *„At college"*, *„Information about people"* und *„Work"*.

Um Ihnen das Vokabellernen zu erleichtern, bietet Ihnen dieses Heft als Lerntraining Wortfelder zu wichtigen Themenbereichen aus dem gesamten Lehrbuch. In jeder Wortliste erscheinen Vokabeln aus der jeweiligen Unit sowie Wörter aus anderen Teilen des Lehrwerks, die mit einem Punkt (˙) gekennzeichnet sind, zum Beispiel ˙*to pass* auf Seite 5. Dann folgen abwechslungsreiche Aufgaben, in denen Sie das Vokabular festigen und im Kontext anwenden. Das letzte Kapitel enthält ausschließlich Wortfelder zu Themenbereichen des Sozialwesens.

Als weiteren Service finden Sie *talking vocabulary* unter www.klett.de: Alle Wortfelder stehen Ihnen hier im MP3-Format zur Verfügung, damit Sie die Aussprache hören und üben können.

Ebenfalls über einen Online-Link – 800037-0040 – erhalten Sie die berufsspezifischen Vokabeln zu den Bereichen Wirtschaft, Technik und Sozialwesen.

Für die Erweiterung Ihres Wortschatzes und die Vorbereitung auf Ihre Prüfungen wünschen wir Ihnen viel Erfolg.

Ihr *Freeway*-Team

Unit 1

Young people in Europe

At college		
Health and Social Care	Gesundheits- und Sozialwesen	care for children or old/sick people
social care	Sozialwissenschaft, Sozialwesen	→ to care
social studies	Sozialwesen, Sozialkunde	→ social → study
National Diploma	zweijähriges Studium am College	e.g. National Diploma in Health and Social Care
further education	höhere Schulbildung, Aus- und Weiterbildung	You can get further education at a college.
Science	Wissenschaft	Biology, Chemistry, Physics
Geography	Geographie	a subject in which you learn about different countries
Biology	Biologie	a subject in which you learn about plants and animals
Physics	Physik	a subject in which you learn about matter and energy
project	Projekt, Vorhaben	e.g. an environmental project
presentation	Präsentation	→ presenter → to present
essay	Aufsatz	a short text by a student
to achieve	erreichen	to reach an aim; → achievement
to pass	bestehen	to be successful in an exam
to fail	durchfallen, versagen	→ failure ↔ to pass
term	Trimester	In Britain, a school year is divided into three terms.
leaver	Schulabgänger(in)	→ to leave

= synonym ↔ opposite → word family

Online Link
800037-0001

Information about people

country of origin	Herkunftsland	the country you were born in
nationality	Nationalität	→ nation → national
citizenship	Staatsangehörigkeit, Nationalität	→ citizen
residence	Wohnsitz	→ to reside
marital status	Ehestand, Familienstand	if s.o. is married or single; → married, to get married
gender	Geschlecht	male or female gender
to be aged	im Alter sein	→ age
under-age	minderjährig	legally too young to do certain things
adult	Erwachsene(r)	= grown-up; → adulthood → adult *(adj.)*
personality	Persönlichkeit	→ person
lifestyle	Lebensstil	the way you live your life
behaviour	Verhalten	→ to behave
attitude (to/towards)	Haltung	a feeling or an opinion about people or things
membership	Mitgliedschaft	→ member
convinced	überzeugt	→ conviction
religion	Religion, Glaube	→ religious
campaigning	Aktionen; Wahlkampf führen	→ campaign → to campaign
aim	Ziel	= goal, target
dislike	Abneigung	↔ like → to dislike
habit	Gewohnheit, Angewohnheit	s.th. a person does often or regularly
impression	Eindruck	→ to impress
identity	Identität	who a person really is
subculture	Subkultur	→ subcultural
condition	Kondition, Zustand	e.g. the condition of being rich
to settle	sich einleben, sich niederlassen	to go and live somewhere, often permanently

= synonym ↔ opposite → word family

Work		
workplace	Arbeitsplatz	→ work → worker → to work
part-time job	Teilzeitjob	↔ full-time job
placement	Praktikum	a job where you can get some work experience
· apprenticeship	Ausbildung	→ apprentice
· trainee	Praktikant(in), Auszubildende(r)	→ traineeship → training → to train
· nine-to-five job	geregelter Arbeitstag	a job with regular working hours
sales talk	Verkaufsgespräch	a talk in which s.o. sells s.th.
to take orders	Bestellungen entgegen-nehmen	e.g. Waiters and waitresses take orders.
· on duty	im Dienst	e.g. the receptionist on duty
· workshop	Werkstatt	→ work → to work
to assist	assistieren, helfen	→ assistance → assistant
to monitor	beaufsichtigen, beobachten	= to observe
to aid	helfen	→ aid
· replacement	Ersatz, Vertretung	= substitute; → to replace
· complicated	kompliziert	↔ easy
· colleague	Kollege/Kollegin	a person who works with you
· workmate	Kollege/Kollegin	a person who works with you
· managing director	Geschäftsführer(in), Mitglied der Geschäftsführung	→ management → to manage
· staff	Belegschaft, Kollegium	the people who work for a company, school etc.
· operative	angelernte(r) Arbeiter(in)	a skilled worker; → to operate
· day off	arbeitsfreier Tag	day without work
· driving licence *(BE)*	Führerschein	driver's licence *(AE)*
· feedback	Rückmeldung, Feedback	e.g. getting feedback on your work performance
· practicability	Durchführbarkeit, Praktikabilität	→ to practise → practical, practicable

= synonym ↔ opposite → word family

Exercises

1 Read the clues and complete the grid.

1 A subject in which you study Biology, Chemistry, and Physics
2 When you work on a particular subject at college over a period of time, you do a …
3 If you don't pass a test or an exam, you …
4 Someone who has finished school
5 A talk in which you give information about something, for example about the results of a project you did at school or college
6 A subject at school or college in which you learn about different countries
7 A short text written by a student, especially as part of the work for a course

		1											
	2												
3													
			4	l	e	a	v	e	r				
	5												
			6	G	e	o	g	r	a	p	h	ie	
			7	e	s	s	a	y					

2 Word families: Fill in the corresponding nouns or verbs.

Noun	Verb
impression	
	to reside
campaigning	
	to fail
trainee	
	to dislike
replacement	
	to manage
practicability	

Noun	Verb
leaver	leave
	to behave
presentation	
	to achieve
studies	
	to work
assistant	
	to aid
operative	

3 **Complete these sentences with words and phrases from page 6.**

a) Your .... is the way you live your life.

b) A culture within a culture is called a ....

c) The country you were born in is your ....

d) Islam is a world ....

e) A person's .... is the situation or state he or she is in.

f) People under 18 are ....

g) If you .... in another country, you go and live there permanently.

4 **Match the words on the left with the definitions on the right. Write down the right letters below.**

1	marital status	A	a strong opinion
2	aim	B	a feeling or an opinion about people or things
3	personality	C	belonging to an organization or group
4	conviction	D	something you want to achieve
5	gender	E	something a person does often or regularly
6	attitude	F	who or what you really are
7	habit	G	if a person is married or single
8	membership	H	the condition of being male or female
9	identity	I	all the important aspects of a person's character

1	2	3	4	5	6	7	8	9

5 **Write down synonyms.**

citizenship – .... replacement – ....

to monitor – .... workmate – ....

6 Complete the statements by young people from Britain with these words.

staff | nine-to-five job | placement | Health and Social Care | day | colleagues | sales talks | part-time job | apprenticeship | orders | National Diploma | on duty | further education | workplace

Brendan, 20, from Newcastle: "I'm doing a .... in applied social studies at a college of .... because I would like to help people in my job later. At the moment I'm doing a .... in a youth club. I don't mind working in the evenings or at the weekend. I don't need a ...."

Germaine, 19, from Bristol: "I think old people need our love and attention, so I've decided to study .... At the weekends I work in a nursing home for the elderly. It's a good .... to get some experience."

Damian, 21, from York: "Last year I started an .... as a waiter. I'm working in a very busy restaurant and have to take lots of .... In a restaurant, the kitchen .... and the waiters have to work together in an organized way."

Rachel, 19, from Edinburgh: "To finance my flat I have a .... in a small boutique. I am usually .... from 10am to 3pm three times a week. Sometimes I do more hours if I have to cover for one of my .... when they have a .... off. My boss says I'm good at making ...."

Unit 2

Working in a social environment

Applying for a job		
application	Bewerbung	→ applicant → to apply
curriculum vitae	Lebenslauf	= CV = resumé
requirement	Anforderung	→ to require → requisite
advert	Anzeige	→ advertisement → to advertise
agency	Agentur	e.g. recruitment agency; → agent
candidate	Bewerber(in)	s.o. who is trying to get a job
vacancy	Stellenangebot	→ vacant
on a yearly basis	jahrweise, ein Jahr	for one year at a time
reputation	Ansehen, Ruf	→ reputable
short-term	kurzfristig	↔ long-term
challenge	Herausforderung	→ to challenge → challenging
essential	wichtig	= very important
relevant	relevant, bedeutend	→ relevance; ↔ irrelevant
aspect	Aspekt, Gesichtspunkt	a particular part of s.th.
demanding	anspruchsvoll, schwierig	→ demand → to demand
beneficial	nützlich, förderlich	= useful; → benefit
equivalent	vergleichbar mit	e.g. *Fachhochschulreife* is equivalent to British A levels.
to enclose	beifügen	→ enclosure
to trust	vertrauen	to believe that s.o. is honest; → trustworthy
to cancel	absagen	→ cancellation
rejection	Ablehnung, Absage	→ to reject

= synonym ↔ opposite → word family

Online Link
800037-0002

Abilities and qualities		
qualification	Qualifikation	→ to qualify (for) → qualified
ability	Fähigkeit	→ able ↔ inability
fluency	Sprachbeherrschung	→ fluent
active	aktiv	→ action → activity → to act
reliable	zuverlässig	→ reliability → to rely (on)
˙truthful	ehrlich	= honest
responsible	verantwortlich, verantwortungsbewusst	→ responsibility
˙resilient	belastbar, stabil, robust	→ resilience
suitable	geeignet	→ suitability → to suit ↔ unsuitable
˙talent	Talent, Begabung	→ talented
˙potential	Potential, Leistungsvermögen	the possibility to develop or achieve s.th. in the future
musical	musikalisch	→ music
˙creative	kreativ	→ creativity → to create
˙discipline	Disziplin	→ to discipline → disciplined
˙eager	eifrig	→ eagerness
˙self-confidence	Selbstbewusstsein	→ self-confident

Exercises

1 Work out the anagrams and write down the words.

a) Burt will probably go in for a career. He has great TENPILOTA. ....

b) Bridget's LYBITIA to stay calm even in difficult situations is amazing. ....

c) I applied for a job with a hospital but I received a JOICENTRE. ....

d) Good manners are TALESESIN in a job interview. ....

e) It will be FIABELECIN to write down all the VALTREEN SCAPTES you are interested in.

....

f) A National Diploma in Health and Social Care is AVETIQUELN to three A levels.

....

= synonym ↔ opposite → word family

2 Word families: Fill in the corresponding words.

Noun	Verb	Adjective
action		
	to challenge	
		reliable
creativity		
	to require	
		demanding
discipline		
	to qualify (for)	
		suitable

3 What do these words mean? Tick the right answer.

challenge:
a) a situation in which something becomes different ☐
b) something that is difficult and tests your ability and skill ☐
c) something that is dangerous and tests your ability to react fast ☐

fluency:
a) the ability to speak and write a foreign language easily, well and quickly ☐
b) permanent change in your life ☐
c) the ability to learn foreign languages very fast ☐

self-confidence:
a) the quality of people who think they can achieve more than others ☐
b) believing in yourself, your abilities and your knowledge ☐
c) the ability to do things on your own, not needing help from other people ☐

requirement:
a) presents you want from other people ☐
b) something that you must have if you want to do a certain thing ☐
c) the same as 'qualification' ☐

reputation:
a) conservative political opinions and beliefs ☐
b) strong dislike of people because they have behaved badly ☐
c) the opinion other people have about you ☐

4 Translate the words below and find them in the grid. One word has been given to help you get started. → ← ↓ ↑

1 Verantwortung
2 Agentur
3 Stellenangebot
4 Ablehnung
5 Lebenslauf
6 beigefügt
7 Anzeige
8 Eifer
9 Bewerbung
10 langfristig
11 erforderlich
12 begabt
13 Bewerber(in)
14 qualifiziert
15 aktiv

A	E	A	G	E	R	N	E	S	S	N	U	H	K	Y	M	U	E	Y
P	B	E	A	T	I	V	M	U	L	U	C	I	R	R	U	C	D	C
P	P	Y	C	T	J	S	M	R	E	T	G	N	O	L	I	W	E	N
L	B	R	A	G	E	N	C	Y	N	Q	E	V	I	T	C	A	S	A
I	S	E	K	E	F	D	R	M	J	E	W	P	F	U	A	D	O	C
C	C	A	N	D	I	D	A	T	E	W	K	U	E	M	J	H	L	A
A	M	R	K	L	Y	G	H	N	O	I	T	C	E	J	E	R	C	V
T	O	D	E	T	N	E	L	A	T	O	B	C	L	W	E	Q	N	F
I	G	Y	Y	T	I	L	I	B	I	S	N	O	P	S	E	R	E	S
O	A	D	V	E	R	T	E	C	Y	Q	U	A	L	I	F	I	E	D
N	P	S	Y	R	L	E	T	I	S	I	U	Q	E	R	E	F	L	D

5 Write down adjectives that characterize these people.

a) James is always honest. He is a .... person.

b) Elisa is very .... She can sing beautifully and she is also a good pianist.

c) Mr Richards never forgets any task he has been given. His boss thinks he is extremely

....

d) Miranda wants people to like her. She is .... to please.

e) Jason has always loved to draw and paint, and by now he has developed into quite

a .... young artist.

Unit 3

Young people as consumers

Consumption		
consumer	Konsument(in), Verbraucher(in)	→ consumption → to consume
to purchase	kaufen	→ purchase
auction	Versteigerung	e.g. You can buy things cheaply in an auction.
bid	Gebot	e.g. winning bid; → to bid
payment	Bezahlung	→ to pay
to try on	anprobieren	to put on clothes in order to see if they fit
to exchange	umtauschen, austauschen	e.g. This CD doesn't work. I'd like to exchange it.
to change one's mind	seine Meinung ändern	to decide differently
packaging	Verpackungsmaterial	→ to pack
to unpack	auspacken	↔ to pack
discount	Rabatt, Nachlass	= reduced price
ˈrange	Angebot, Produktpalette	→ to range
ˈon offer	im Angebot	e.g. There is 50% off the shoes. They are on offer.
ˈinexpensive	preiswert, billig	= cheap; ↔ expensive
ˈmust-have	etwas Unentbehrliches, ein Muss	e.g. this season's must-haves for any woman
ˈfashionable	modisch	→ fashion ↔ unfashionable
ˈtrendy	modisch, trendig	→ trend
silver	Silber	e.g. This ring is made of silver.
ˈaccessory	Zubehör, Accessoire	e.g. a scarf or a handbag

= synonym ↔ opposite → word family

Online Link
800037-0003

Trading and advertising		
advertiser	Inserent(in), Werbefachmann/-frau	→ advertising → advertisement → to advertise
agency	Agentur	e.g. advertising agency
promotion	Werbung, Promotion	→ to promote
marketing	Marketing	→ to market
merchandising	Verkaufsförderung, Merchandising, Vermarktung	e.g. In a merchandising campaign a football club sells products with the club's logo.
sponsoring	Sponsoring, Förderung, finanzielle Unterstützung	→ a sponsor → to sponsor
distribution	Vertrieb	→ to distribute
logo	Firmenemblem	a design or symbol a company uses on its products
no-name product	Billigprodukt, Produkt ohne Markennamen	↔ branded product
uniqueness	Einzigartigkeit	→ unique
target	Ziel	= aim, goal; → to target
commercial	Werbespot	During TV shows there are commercials for cars, coffee, …
slogan	Slogan, Werbespruch	a short phrase that a company uses to advertise its products
jingle	Jingle, kurze Tonfolge in der Werbung	a short melody which is easy to remember
flyer	Flugblatt	→ to fly
billboard	Plakatwand, Werbetafel	a board on which posters and adverts are displayed outdoors
to persuade	überreden	→ persuasion → persuasive
trader	Händler(in)	→ trade → to trade
to be based	Geschäftssitz haben	e.g. The company is based in London.
to label	kennzeichnen, etikettieren	→ label
to create	schaffen	→ creation → creativity → creative

= synonym ↔ opposite → word family

Mobile phones		
mobile phone	Mobiltelefon, Handy	= mobile, cellphone *(AE)*; → to phone s.o.
mobile	mobil, beweglich	→ mobility
˙electronic	elektronisch	e.g. A mobile phone is an electronic device.
˙telecommunications	Telekommunikation	→ communications → to communicate
text message	Textmitteilung, SMS	SMS = short message service
premium rate number	Sonderrufnummer	telephone number for calls during which special services are provided
to delete	löschen	→ deletion
ringtone	Klingelton	e.g. My best friend has his favourite song as a ringtone on his mobile phone.
wallpaper	Hintergrundbild; Tapete	e.g. My boyfriend has my picture as a wallpaper on his mobile.
alert	Alarm	a signal that warns of a danger; → to alert
short code	Kurzwahlnummer	e.g. To get the latest football news send an SMS with 'football' to the short code 72404.
˙feature	Einrichtung, Eigenschaft	= characteristic; e.g. features of mobile phones
˙battery	Batterie, Akku	a device that you put inside a clock, radio, mobile phone etc. which produces electricity
˙to reload	wieder aufladen	to load again, to top up; e.g. to reload a prepaid phone card
˙credit	Guthaben	e.g. I can't phone Emily because I've got no credit on my mobile.
˙instant	sofort	An instant message is a message you get right away.
˙operator	Betreiber(in)	→ operation → to operate; e.g. mobile phone operator

= synonym ↔ opposite → word family

Law and regulations		
right	Recht	e.g. Children don't have the right to drive cars. It's illegal.
regulation	Regel, Vorschrift	an official rule; → to regulate
contract	Vertrag	a legal agreement between two people or groups
to agree in a contract	einen Vertrag abschließen	to sign a contract
confirmation	Bestätigung	→ to confirm
cooling-off period	Widerspruchsfrist	the period during which a buyer can get his money back
scam	Betrug	a clever illegal plan to make money; → to scam
crime	Verbrechen, Kriminalität	e.g. to commit a serious crime, a high crime rate; → criminal
˙to prove	beweisen	to show that s.th. is true
˙evidence	Beweis, Beweismaterial	s.th. that makes s.th. clear or that proves s.th.; → evident
ban	Verbot	→ to ban
˙penalty	Strafe	= punishment
˙offender	Angreifer(in), Täter(in)	s.o. who has done s.th. wrong; → offence → to offend

Exercises

1 Word building: Write down the corresponding nouns for activities. What do they all have in common? Are there any differences?

to distribute .... to regulate ....

to promote .... to delete ....

to create .... to operate ....

....

= synonym ↔ opposite → word family

2 **Find eight noun-verb pairs in the lists on pages 15 to 18 that have the same forms.**

Noun	Verb

Noun	Verb

3 **Use some words from exercise 2 to fill in the gaps.**

a) Marketers use clever methods to .... children in commercials.

b) As kids have difficulties distinguishing between advertising and reality, parents' organizations call for a .... on all advertising aimed at children.

c) Mr Taylor lost a lot of money in an insurance ....

d) In case of fire you have to .... the fire brigade as quickly as possible.

e) Designer .... clothing is mostly bought by the upper-middle class.

f) Before you place a .... in an Internet auction, you should become familiar with the auction site and find out about its rules.

g) In a superstore you can find a huge .... of products.

h) The software company announced its $30 million .... of one of its major competitors.

4 **Mark the word in each row that does not go with the others. Explain your choice.**

a) marketing – distribution – trendy – consumption ....

b) text message – ringtone – operator – wallpaper ....

c) scam – ban – penalty – regulation ....

d) commercial – auction – jingle – advertisement ....

e) trader – consumer – flyer – advertiser ....

5 Read the clues and fill in the grid.

1 When something is on offer you can buy it at a …
2 A product that many people want to have
3 A person who buys something in order to use it on their own
4 The act of paying money for something
5 The same as 'cheap'
6 A white metal that is used for making coins, rings, knives and forks
7 Popular and trendy
8 Paper, plastic or other materials around products that are sold in shops

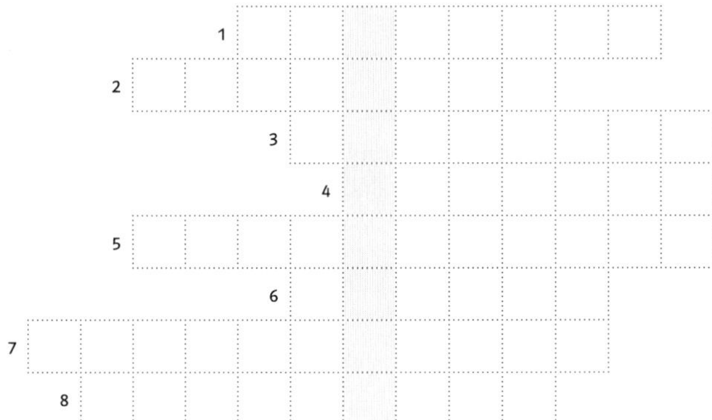

6 Complete the words.

a) Before a company starts to c … t … a brand it must identify the possible costumers so that p … m … t … of its products will be effective.

b) A unique business l … g … is essential for successful m … ch … d … .

c) Big companies often use sp … r … as a tool of m … t … g.

d) So-called n … -n … m … p … d … s are usually distinguished from b … d … d p … d … s, although most of them have a name, which is just lesser-known and not ad … e … t … ed.

e) B … b … ds can typically be found on the sides of busy roads and present large a … e … t … m … s, often with original s … o … s, to pedestrians and drivers.

f) A lot of famous a … v … t … s … ng a … c … s are b … s … d in London.

7 Complete the sentences with these expressions.

premium rate number | wallpapers | credit | battery

reload | short codes | features | text messages

electronic | ringtones | instant | telecommunications

a) Young children don't need mobile phones with a lot of different ....

b) Giving children prepaid mobile phones is a good way to teach them how to be responsible with their ....

c) Parents can refuse to .... the phones for a while if the children have used them too often.

d) .... involve voice, video and Internet services.

e) A survey done in 2009 showed that over 50% of American teenagers send at least 50 .... per day.

f) A lot of young adults like to personalize their mobile phones by downloading .... with complicated melodies or .... with unusual images.

g) .... messaging is a form of real-time communication.

h) An e-book is a book published in .... form.

i) Oh no, my mobile says "Low ...." and I left my charger at home!

j) Before calling a .... find out how much you will be charged.

k) .... are easier to read and remember than other phone numbers.

8 **Match the sentence parts.**

1. An offender is a person
2. If you agree in a contract
3. It is a basic human right
4. A penalty is
5. If you want to prove a crime
6. During a cooling-off period

a) a punishment for an action that is against the law.
b) a customer can return a product.
c) you need clear evidence.
d) who commits a crime.
e) to think and speak freely.
f) you sign it.

1. 2. 3. 4. 5. 6.

9 **Complete the definitions with words and phrases from this unit. Sometimes you have to use plural forms.**

a) A ______ is a statement saying that a meeting is certain.

b) A ______ thing is the only one of its kind.

c) Something that is ______ is sold at a discount.

d) ______ are companies that create different forms of promotion for their clients.

e) ______ are things you add to your outfits to make them look more stylish.

10 **Fill in verbs and verb phrases from this unit.**

If you …

a) … make people do something, you ______ them.

b) … want to find out if a piece of clothing fits you, you have to ______ it ______.

c) … give a product back and get a new one instead, you ______ the product.

d) … decide differently, you ______.

e) … take things out of a box or a parcel, you ______ them.

Unit 4

Living with the media

Computers		
screen	Bildschirm	= monitor
desktop	Desktop, Benutzeroberfläche	the background image on your computer screen
web	Netz	*(short form of)* World Wide Web
browser	Browser	→ to browse
messaging service	Dienst zur Sofortversendung von Nachrichten	e.g. ICQ and Skype are instant messaging services.
icon	Icon, Bildschirmsymbol	e.g. menu icon, trash can icon
to click	klicken	→ click
to update	aktualisieren	→ update
button	Knopf, Taste	e.g. Press the left mouse button.
to download	herunterladen	→ download
file	Datei	e.g. Don't forget to save the file!
wireless	drahtlos	→ wire; WLAN = wireless local area network
programming language	Programmiersprache	→ program → programmer → to program
games console	Spielekonsole	an electronic device used to play video games
provider	Anbieter	→ provision → to provide
keypad	Tastatur	= keyboard
· TLD (top-level domain)	Bereich oberster Ebene	The last letters of an Internet address show its top-level domain, e.g. 'de' for Germany.
· data	Daten	facts, items of information

= synonym ↔ opposite → word family

Online Link
800037-0004

Talking and writing		
conclusion	Schlussfolgerung	→ to conclude
to summarize	zusammenfassen	→ summary
to sum up	zusammenfassen	to explain a text in a few sentences
to comment	kommentieren, Stellung nehmen	to give one's opinion on s.th.; → comment
to propose	vorschlagen	→ proposal
report	Bericht	→ reporter → to report
analysis	Analyse	→ to analyze
to point out	hinweisen auf	If you point out a fact, you tell s.o. about it.
pros and cons	Argumente für und gegen etwas	= advantages and disadvantages
to suggest	vorschlagen	= to propose; → suggestion
context	Kontext, Zusammenhang	the text that comes before and after a particular text passage
Crime and justice		
to steal	stehlen	to take s.th. without permission and keep it
killing	Tötung	→ killer → to kill
murder	Mord	→ murderer → to murder
piracy	Piraterie, Raubkopieren	→ pirate
witness	Zeugin, Zeuge	→ to witness
illegal	illegal, gesetzeswidrig	↔ legal
responsible (for)	verantwortlich (für), haftbar	→ to hold s.o. responsible for s.th. → responsibility
to observe	beobachten	to watch carefully; → observation
to punish	bestrafen	→ punishment
prison	Gefängnis	a building where criminals must live as a punishment
court	Gericht	Before people are sent to prison, they have to appear in court.
judge	Richter	a person who decides in court

= synonym ↔ opposite → word family

1 Read the clues and fill in the crossword.

Across:

3 Items of information
5 The latest improvements to a computer programme
6 Not using wires
8 The same as 'keyboard'
9 The short form of 'World Wide Web'
12 A small object that you press to make a machine or computer work
13 Information that you store on your computer under a particular name
14 A language that makes computers work
15 Another word for 'monitor'

Down:

1 An electronic device used to play video games
2 The highest level of domain names on the Internet
4 Sending a message over a computer network using software that immediately shows the message
7 A small symbol on a computer screen
10 The background image on your computer screen
11 A company that makes Internet services available to users, often a phone or cable company

2 **Word families: Fill in the corresponding nouns or verbs.**

Noun	Verb
browser	
	to click
killing	
	to witness
comment	
	to conclude

Noun	Verb
	to summarize
download	
	to propose
report	
	to suggest
analysis	

3 **Complete the sentences with these words.**

point out · summary · suggest · pros and cons · context · proposal · analysis · comment

a) A ________ is an essay in which you first discuss some important ________ of a statement or a thesis and then give your opinion.

b) You can easily understand new words and phrases if you look closely at the ________.

c) A ________ is a short text in which you present in your own words the most important aspects of a text that you have read.

d) In a cartoon ________ you explain what the cartoonist wants to ________.

e) If you are against the introduction of CCTV at this college, you have to be able to ________ good alternatives.

f) A debate is a discussion in which you give reasons for and against a ________.

4 **Finish the definitions.**

a) A judge is a person who ……………………

b) A murderer is a person who ……………………

c) A reporter is a person who ……………………

5 **Read the text and work out the anagrams. Write down the correct words below. Then add the German translations.**

The film and music industries say that (1) CRYPIA on the Internet is costing them billions of dollars. One in four Internet users admits to having (2) WENDODODAL films. This is an act of (3) NEGLASIT called copyright theft. (4) GLALILE copying of digital entertainment has become an immense problem all over the world and a rapid increase is being (5) VEDBORES. A lot of states now hold copyright thieves (6) SORPILEBNES and (7) SIPUHN them with tough penalties. (8) TRUCSO have also convicted operators of so-called BitTorrent trackers, which are Internet services providing links to songs, films, video games and other material and helping users to download (9) SIFEL. Some of these people were sent to (10) SORNIP and had to pay damages to leading entertainment companies.

(1) …………………… ……………………

(2) …………………… ……………………

(3) …………………… ……………………

(4) …………………… ……………………

(5) …………………… ……………………

(6) …………………… ……………………

(7) …………………… ……………………

(8) …………………… ……………………

(9) …………………… ……………………

(10) …………………… ……………………

Unit 5

Developments in society

Work		
wage	Lohn	money that is paid for work
salary	Gehalt	money that is paid every month for work
profession	Beruf	e.g. the profession of teaching; → professional
commitment	Engagement, Verpflichtung, Bekenntnis	When you work towards s.th. you show your commitment to it.
opportunity	Gelegenheit	= chance; e.g. job opportunities
unpaid	unbezahlt	↔ paid
voluntary	freiwillig, ehrenamtlich	→ volunteering → volunteer → to volunteer
labour	Arbeits-	= work; → labour *(n.)*
organizational	organisatorisch	→ organization → to organize
mechanical	mechanisch, technisch	→ mechanic
motivation	Motivation, Leistungsbereitschaft	→ to motivate → motivated
routine	Routine, Tagesablauf	regular tasks in a fixed order
task	Aufgabe	a piece of work that is difficult or that you don't enjoy doing
shift	(Arbeits-)Schicht	a period of work
function	Funktion, Aufgabe(nbereich)	= role, purpose, task; → to function → functional
conference	Konferenz	a meeting to discuss s.th.
to interact	interagieren, zusammenwirken	→ interaction → interactive

= synonym ↔ opposite → word family

Online Link
800037-0005

Women, partnership and family		
missus	umgangssprachliche Anrede für eine Frau	→ Mrs
pregnancy	Schwangerschaft	→ pregnant
feminist	Feministin, Frauenrechtlerin	→ feminism
female	weiblich	↔ male
beauty	Schönheit	→ beautiful
contraception	Schwangerschafts-verhütung	→ contraceptive
engaged	verlobt	having agreed to marry s.o.; → engagement → to become engaged
· relationship	Beziehung	the way in which two people behave and feel towards each other
affair	Affäre	a secret sexual relationship
condom	Kondom	You can have safer sex if you use a condom.
· impotence	Impotenz, Zeugungs-unfähigkeit	→ impotent
· marriage	Heirat, Hochzeit	→ to marry → married
· wedding	Hochzeit	e.g. Paul and Jane really love each other. Their wedding is on Friday.
· honeymoon	Hochzeitsreise	journey after one's wedding
single parent	Alleinerziehende(r)	= lone parent
single mum	alleinerziehende Mutter	woman who is a single parent
· to raise	großziehen	e.g. Parents raise their children until they are grown up.
· childcare	Kinderbetreuung	care for children provided by the government or institutions
· grandchild	Enkelkind, Enkel(in)	→ grandson → granddaughter
· demographic	demographisch, bevölkerungsstatistisch	→ demographics
· generation	Generation	e.g. the older generation

= synonym ↔ opposite → word family

School		
comprehensive school	Gesamtschule	schools for people from 11 to 16 or 18 years old
special needs	Förderschul-	Special needs teachers can help pupils with learning difficulties.
nursery school	Vorschule	a school for children between three and five years of age
primary school	Grundschule	the first school you go to
secondary school	weiterführende Schule	high school
residential school	Internat	school which offers accommodation to students
head teacher *(BE)*	Schulleiter(in)	principal *(AE)*
class time	Unterrichtszeit	= lessons
mark	Zensur	= grade
coaching	Nachhilfeunterricht, Coaching	special classes, often private, given to one person or to a small group
certificate	Zeugnis, Urkunde, Bescheinigung, Zertifikat	When you pass an exam, you will get a certificate.
GCSE	Prüfung zum Abschluss der Sekundarstufe	General Certificate of Secondary Education
campus	Campus, (Hoch-) Schulgelände	area of land with the buildings of a university or school
yard	Hof	an area outside a building
courtyard	(Innen-)Hof	a flat, open area with buildings around it
corridor	Gang, Flur, Korridor	= hall, hallway
canteen	Kantine, Mensa	a place in a school where people can sit and eat
library	Bibliothek	a place where you can read and borrow books without payment
gym	Sporthalle	= sports hall
exchange	Austausch	e.g. an international school exchange
educational	lehrreich, bildend	→ education

= synonym ↔ opposite → word family

Exercises

1 Word building: Add the right endings to the nouns.

-ion -ation -ary -ship -ment -ity -ism

relation ....

opportun ....

motiv ....

interact ....

funct ....

organiz ....

profess ....

femin ....

sal ....

educ ....

contracept ....

commit ....

2 Word families: Fill in the corresponding nouns or adjectives.

Noun	Adjective
pregnancy	
	voluntary
marriage	
	beautiful
interaction	
	demographic

Noun	Adjective
mechanic	
	functional
labour	
	impotent
engagement	
	male

3 Write down the German translations and add synonyms.

	German	Synonym
gym		
opportunity		
single parent		
class time		
mark		
corridor		

4 **Collocations: Combine the verbs from the left box with the phrases from the right box. Write down all the possible combinations.**

to be • to get • to have • to become	a conference • pregnant • married • a relationship • engaged • a low wage • good marks • a high salary • an affair

....

....

....

....

....

Now explain why 'become' is a false friend.

....

5 **Complete the words. You can find all of them on page 29.**

a) C__n__a__p__n helps people to prevent unwanted __r__n__c__s.

b) Using c__d__s immensely lowers the risk of being infected with HIV.

c) Since the 19th century f__i__ activists have fought for women's rights.

d) No one has counted yet all the many poems on __e__a__b__y.

e) In western societies nowadays not many couples get e__g__ before they m__y.

f) However, a lot of them want to have a formal, pompous w__d__ and at least one week of __o__m__.

g) The daily lives of s__g__m__s can be very stressful.

h) Most of them have to work and need good ch__c__.

i) Those who can at least rely on grandparents' help in r__s__g their kids are better off than others.

j) A lot of elderly people enjoy spending time with their g__dch__ld__.

6 **Complete the sentences with these words.**

shift | motivation | commitment (2x) | organizational | conference | opportunities | organized | professions | interact | labour | tasks | unpaid | routine | mechanical

a) Medicine, nursing, law, teaching and engineering are ______________.

b) Voluntary work is a form of social ______________ and it is ______________.

c) In a basic ______________ skills seminar you learn how to use different tools.

d) Why don't Western European governments do more to keep foreign students in their ______________ markets?

e) The job ______________ in health care management will be very good in the next few years.

f) ______________ work is physically demanding, especially if you have to work at night.

g) Jason's daily ______________ is strictly ______________ around his studies.

h) People who are satisfied with their jobs have a high ______________ to work and be successful, whereas people who have to work under difficult conditions often do not show much ______________ when performing their ______________.

i) Studies also show that people who ______________ well at their workplace are usually able to achieve their individual and ______________ goals.

j) Last weekend representatives from all continents attended a ______________ on working conditions for women in different parts of the world.

7 Read the clues and fill in the grid.

1 A place in a school where you can have lunch
2 A place outside that is surrounded by buildings
3 The first school you go to is the ... school.
4 A ... school is a school where pupils live and study.
5 The qualification you receive when you have passed an exam
6 British ... schools are similar to German *Gesamtschulen.*
7 A place in town or in a school where you can borrow books, CDs and DVDs
8 The British system of taking examinations at the age of about 16
9 An area of land with the buildings of a university or school
10 In a student ... a school sends pupils to a partner school and receives pupils from there as guests.
11 Special private classes for pupils who have problems in certain subjects
12 ... schools are high schools.
13 ... schools cater to children with disabilities or learning difficulties.

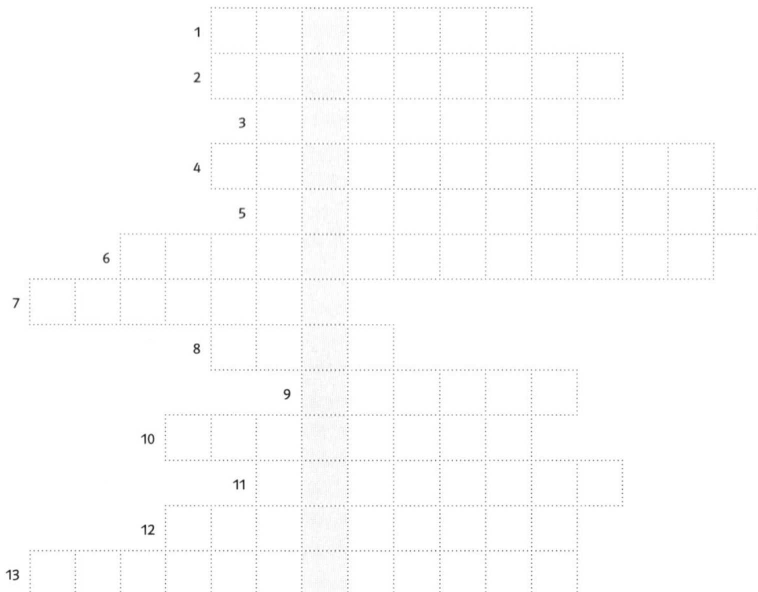

Unit 6

Environment and education

Nature		
natural	natürlich	→ nature ↔ unnatural
rainfall	Niederschlag, Regen	rain + fall = rainfall
rainforest	Regenwald	rain + forest = rainforest
resource	Ressource, Bodenschatz, Rohstoff	e.g. It is important not to waste the world's natural resources.
to run out	ablaufen, auslaufen, zu Ende gehen	e.g. Will the earth run out of resources by 2050?
crystal	Kristall	a mineral (e.g. diamond) that has a regular shape
gas	Gas, Benzin	any substance like air; gas *(AE)* = petrol *(BE)*
nuclear	nuklear, Atom-	= atomic; e.g. nuclear waste
wave	Welle	When there is a storm at sea there are huge waves.
algae *pl.*	Algen, Tang	plants that live in the water
desert	Wüste	It doesn't rain often in the desert.
countryside	Landschaft, Land	e.g. Britain's beautiful countryside, living in the countryside
wild	wild	e.g. wild animals
wildlife	Tierwelt (in freier Wildbahn)	all animals that don't live in zoos, people's homes or on farms
organism	Organismus	e.g. an animal or a plant
creature	Kreatur, Lebewesen	a living thing
to explore	erkunden	e.g. to explore a place
to be equipped	ausgestattet, ausgerüstet sein	→ equipment

= synonym ↔ opposite → word family

Online Link
800037-0006

Environment		
· environmental	Umwelt-	e.g. environmental organization
ecology	Ökologie	→ ecological
to recycle	recyceln, wiederverwerten	→ recycling → to recycle → recyclable
global	global	relating to the whole world
warming	Erwärmung	→ warm
fossil fuel	fossiler Brennstoff	Coal and oil are fossil fuels.
to emit	emittieren, ausstoßen	= to give out or send out; → emission
carbon dioxide	Kohlendioxyd, CO_2	You get CO_2 gases when you burn coal or wood.
increasing	zunehmend, steigend, wachsend	→ increase → to increase ↔ decreasing
conservation	Erhaltung, Schutz	→ to conserve
to save	sparen	e.g. to save resources; ↔ to waste
organic	biologisch angebaut, organisch	= natural
water-related disease	Krankheit, die durch (unsauberes) Wasser verursacht wird	e.g. In Africa you find many water-related diseases.
disaster	Katastrophe, Desaster	a very bad accident
catastrophe	Katastrophe	an extremely terrible disaster
overfishing	Überfischung	→ fishing → fish
low-flush toilet	Toilette mit geringem Wasserverbrauch	e.g. You can save water by using low-flush toilets.
sustainable	nachhaltig	e.g. sustainable development
· to exploit	verwerten, ausbeuten	→ exploitation
· harmful	schaden, verletzen	→ to harm
· toxic	giftig	= poisonous
· biofuel	Biotreibstoff	bio(logical) + fuel = biofuel
· bioreserve	(Bio-)Reservat	area where nature is protected
· sewage	Abwasser	dirty waste water

= synonym ↔ opposite → word family

Dealing with problems/commitment		
worry	Sorge, Ärger	→ to worry → worried
concern	Bedenken, Sorge, Anliegen	a feeling of worry; → concerned
·negative	negativ	= bad, harmful; ↔ positive
to identify (with)	herausfinden, (sich) identifizieren (mit)	→ identification
issue	Angelegenheit, Problem	= topic
aspect	Aspekt, Gesichtspunkt	e.g. This aspect of the problem is the most important.
complex	komplex, vielfältig, kompliziert	consisting of many parts; e.g. a complex problem; ↔ simple
conscience	Gewissen, Bewusstsein	sense of what is right and wrong
responsibility	Verantwortung	→ responsible
to aim	anstreben, zielen	→ aim
to contribute	beitragen	→ contribution
to provide s.o. with	jmdn. versorgen mit	e.g. to provide people with water
·assistance	Hilfe	→ assistant → to assist
to benefit (from)	Nutzen ziehen (aus), profitieren (von)	= to profit (from); e.g. to benefit from aid projects
non-profit	gemeinnützig	= non-commercial
foundation	Stiftung	→ to found
to donate	spenden	→ donation
·support	Unterstützung	→ to support
to encourage	unterstützen, fördern, ermutigen	= to support
improvement	Verbesserung	→ to improve
realisation	Verwirklichung, Realisierung, Erkenntnis	e.g. the realisation of a project; → to realise → real
control	Kontrolle	→ to control
to avoid	(ver)meiden	e.g. We have to avoid environmental disasters.
·to prevent	verhindern	→ prevention
·attempt	Versuch	= effort; → to attempt

= synonym ↔ opposite → word family

Food and food production		
menu	Speisekarte	Waiter, what's on the menu today?
seafood	Fisch und Meeresfrüchte	Seafood is healthy.
tuna, *pl.* tuna	Thunfisch	a large fish that lives in warm seas and is caught for food
salmon, *pl.* salmon	Lachs	a tasty kind of fish which looks pink when you cut it open
protein	Protein, Eiweiß	Protein can be found in meat, fish, eggs and milk.
exotic	exotisch	e.g. Curry is an exotic dish.
· rice	Reis	Risotto is made with rice.
· maize *(BE)*	Mais	corn *(AE)*; a tall plant that produces sweetcorn
· vitamin	Vitamin	natural substance necessary for your health
· carbohydrate	Kohlenhydrat	substance which provides the body with energy, e.g. sugar
· mineral	Mineral	a chemical your body needs
· fibre	Faser, Ballaststoff	→ fibrous
· calorie	Kalorie	If you work hard, you use up more calories.
· nutritious	nahrhaft	→ nutrition
· agriculture	Landwirtschaft	= farming
seed	Saat, Samen	A lot of plants grow from seeds.
· harvest	Ernte	→ to harvest
· crop	Feldfrucht, Getreide, Ernte	a plant grown in large amounts
· fertilizer	Dünger, Düngemittel	→ to fertilize
· pest	Schädling, Pflanzenkrankheit	insect that damages plants
· pesticide	Schädlingsbekämpfungsmittel, Pestizid	chemical used to kill harmful insects
· to spray	sprühen	→ spray

= synonym ↔ opposite → word family

1 **Word building: Match the parts of the words from the boxes and form words. One word has been done for you to help you get started.**

~~rain~~ • bio • wild • over • country • sea • rain • bio • carbo

fuel • fishing • side • life • ~~fall~~ • reserve • hydrate • forest • food

rainfall		

2 **Which words from exercise 1 correspond with these definitions?**

a) Catching too many fish in a particular area of the sea: ....

b) Land outside cities and towns with forests, fields and grasslands: ....

c) Animals that live on their own in natural conditions, not near people: ....

d) An area where animals and plants are protected: ....

3 **Write down the opposites.**

negative ↔ ....

to save ↔ ....

complex ↔ ....

increasing ↔ ....

4 **Work out the anagrams and write down the words.**

a) ETARUCER ....

b) VIROCANSENOT ....

c) SARCTYL ....

d) PITLIOXATONE ....

e) LYNCRICEG ....

f) GALEA ....

g) OGELYCO ....

h) STREED ....

i) AGWESE ....

j) VETRONPIMEM ....

5 **Use five words from exercise 4 to complete these sentences.**

a) .... is the study of interactions between organisms, such as plants and animals, with the environment.

b) If we don't stop the .... of nature, there will be even more natural catastrophes such as wild storms and floods in the future.

c) Introducing a low emission zone in our city has been an environmental ....

d) The .... of existing ecosystems is one of the major focuses of environmental organizations and green parties.

e) Well-run .... programs cost less than collecting rubbish and then depositing it in landfills or burning it.

6 **Fill in the gaps with these verb forms.**

aims	harms	identify	run out	contribute	provide

a) How long will the Earth .... us with oil and coal?

b) What will happen if we .... of these fuels in a few decades?

c) Transporting food over long distances .... the environment.

d) Greenpeace .... to preserve the diversity of the Earth.

e) Most people can .... with this goal, but some criticize the organization's direct actions.

f) There are many simple ways in which you can .... to saving energy and protecting nature.

7 **Match the synonyms and write down the pairs.**

disaster | nuclear | issue | to emit | to encourage | to benefit | negative | catastrophe | agriculture | to profit | farming | natural | toxic | atomic | worried | topic | to give out | to assist | to support | bad | organic | poisonous | concerned | to help

8 **Match the sentence parts.**

1. Your responsibility
2. If you need assistance,
3. A concern
4. Complex problems
5. When you are able to realise a plan
6. Most foundations
7. Regular donations of money or goods
8. If you make an attempt,
9. Your conscience tells you

a) are often difficult to solve.
b) you try to do something difficult.
c) are non-profit organizations.
d) someone has to help you.
e) are a form of social commitment.
f) whether actions are good or bad.
g) is your job or your duty.
h) you achieve the result that you expected.
i) is an issue that worries you.

1. 2. 3. 4. 5. 6. 7. 8. 9.

9 **Combine these phrases with the words in the list. Then translate the expressions you have formed into German.**

carbon | global | natural | nuclear | fossil

sustainable | low-flush | non-profit | organic

	fuel	*fossiler Brennstoff*
	toilet	
	farming	
	resources	
	dioxide	
	organization	
	development	
	waste	
	warming	

10 **Translate these phrases.**

a) *gut ausgerüstet sein:*

b) *eine Gegend erkunden:*

c) *hohe Benzinpreise:*

d) *durch Wasser verursachte Krankheiten:*

e) *hohe Wellen:*

f) *Plastik wiederverwerten:*

g) *ein wichtiger Aspekt:*

h) *Risiken vermeiden:*

i) *eine Katastrophe verhindern:*

j) *Geld spenden:*

11 Find words on page 38 to fill in the gaps. You will often need to use plural forms.

a) .... is known as 'corn' in the US and other English-speaking countries.

b) Pineapples and bananas are .... fruit.

c) Fruit, vegetables, nuts and seeds are rich in ...., ... and ....

d) .... cooking keeps you healthy.

e) If you do a sitting job, you don't burn many ....

f) In this bistro, you can find risotto made with organic .... on the ....

g) Fish is high in ...., but environmentalists warn people against eating too many endangered kinds of fish, such as .... or ....

h) If you want to have a beautiful garden in summer, start sowing flower .... in spring.

i) The use of chemical .... in agriculture has increased steadily because they are an effective means of increasing crop production and guaranteeing good ....

j) Organic farmers don't spray .... on their crops, but they use other methods to control ....

Unit 7

Staying healthy in a technological world

Behaviour and emotions		
reaction	Reaktion	→ to react
motive	Beweggrund, Motiv	reason for doing s.th.
emotion	Gefühl, Emotion	→ emotional
to protest	protestieren	→ protest
shocked	schockiert	→ shock → to shock
to upset, upset, upset	aus der Fassung bringen, aufregen	to make s.o. worried or unhappy; → upset *(adj.)*
˙confused	verwirrt	→ confusion
˙resentful	aufgebracht, grollend	→ resentment → to resent
˙hostile	feindlich	→ hostility
˙aggressive	aggressiv, angriffslustig	→ aggression
scepticism	Skepsis, Zweifel	= doubts; → sceptic → sceptical
˙reluctant	zögernd, widerwillig	= unwilling; → reluctance
defiant	trotzig, herausfordernd	→ defiance
˙tension	Anspannung, Spannung	→ tense
˙to fear	fürchten	→ fear
˙anxiety	Angst, Besorgnis	→ anxious
˙frightened	verängstigt	→ to frighten
˙confident	zuversichtlich	→ confidence
˙well-behaved	wohlerzogen, brav	→ behaviour → to behave
˙respect	Respekt	→ to respect → respectful
˙disappointed	enttäuscht	→ disappointment → to disappoint
˙politeness	Höflichkeit	→ polite

= synonym ↔ opposite → word family

Online Link
800037-0007

Biotechnology		
childless	kinderlos	not having any children of one's own
human	menschlich	of people or typical of people; e.g. the human body
being	(Lebe-)Wesen, Geschöpf	→ to be
embryo	Embryo	→ embryonic
to clone	klonen	→ cloning → clone
duplicate	Duplikat, Kopie	= copy; → duplication → to duplicate
biotechnology	Biotechnologie	the use of living organisms e.g. in the production of medicine
biomedical	biomedizinisch	relating to how biology affects medicine
bioengineered	durch Biotechnik geschaffen, genmanipuliert	→ bioengineering
to modify	verändern, modifizieren	→ modification
scientific	wissenschaftlich	→ science → scientist
DNA	DNS, DNA (Träger der Erbinformation)	*(short form of)* deoxyribonucleic acid
lab	Labor(atorium)	*(short form of)* laboratory
genetic	genetisch, Gen-	→ gene
to give birth to	zur Welt bringen, gebären	She gave birth to a sweet little girl.
fertility	Fruchtbarkeit	→ fertile
in-vitro fertilisation	In-vitro-Befruchtung, Befruchtung im Reagenzglas	In-vitro fertilisation (IVF) takes place in a laboratory.
deadly	tödlich	→ death → to die → dead
disease	Krankheit	illness, often caused by infection
GM	gentechnisch verändert, genmanipuliert	*(short form of)* genetically modified
synthetic	synthetisch, künstlich	made of artificial materials, not of natural ones

= synonym ↔ opposite → word family

Body		
breath	Atem, Atemzug	→ to breathe
organ	Organ	part of your body, e.g. your heart
bone marrow	Knochenmark	the inside part of a bone
liver	Leber	an organ
gene	Gen, Erbfaktor	→ genetic
˙stomach	Magen	e.g. You shouldn't go swimming on a full stomach.
˙physical	körperlich, physisch	having to do with the body
˙mental	geistig, mental, seelisch	relating to the mind
˙brain	Gehirn	the organ inside your head that controls your feelings, your thinking and your movements
˙conscious	bewusst, bei Bewusstsein	= aware, awake; → consciousness
˙dehydrated	entwässert, dehydriert	the condition of having lost too much water from your body
˙vomit	Erbrochenes	→ to vomit
Religion and ethics		
God	Gott	→ divine
˙religion	Religion, Glaube	→ religious
˙belief	Glaube, Überzeugung	→ to believe
˙Muslim (*also* Moslem)	Muslim(in)	→ Muslim *(adj.)*
˙Koranic	koranisch, aus dem Koran	related to the Koran
˙Jewish	jüdisch	→ Jew
unethical	unethisch, unmoralisch	= immoral; → ethics ↔ ethical
fate	Schicksal	what happens to you
freedom	Freiheit	→ free
˙tolerance	Toleranz	→ tolerant → to tolerate
˙equality	Gleichheit, Gleichberechtigung	→ equal
˙virtue	Tugend, Rechtschaffenheit	good moral quality of a person; → virtuous

= synonym ↔ opposite → word family

Exercises

1 Word families: Write down the corresponding nouns or adjectives.

Noun	Adjective
embryo	
	defiant
fertility	
	confused
hostility	
	well-behaved
aggression	

Noun	Adjective
science	
	confident
respect	
	conscious
tension	
	disappointed
anxiety	

2 Fill in fitting adjectives.

A person who …

a) … witnesses a horrible scene is ______________.

b) … cries easily is very ______________.

c) … has doubts that something will work out is ______________.

d) … is unwilling to do something is ______________.

e) … has good manners is ______________.

f) … is angry because they have to do something they don't like is ______________.

g) … is ready to argue or behaves aggressively is ______________.

h) … feels fear is ______________.

i) … is very nervous, worried or angry is ______________.

3 **Word families: Write down the corresponding nouns or verbs.**

Noun	Verb
reaction	
	to protest
fear	
	to behave

Noun	Verb
respect	
	to modify
shock	
	to believe

4 **Complete the words. You can find all of them on page 45.**

a) Chinese s__i__n_____s have found a new way of l__n___g cells.

b) They converted skin cells taken from mice into e__br____ic -like cells.

c) Until then it had only been possible to d__p_____t__ animals, but with the new methods specific body tissues can be produced as well now.

d) This has been a breakthrough in b___t____n_____y.

e) At the moment the new techniques are not available to h____n cells, but experts say that it will only be a matter of time until h____n b_____s will be produced.

f) However, a lot of people believe that it should never be possible to produce babies in a l__b________.

5 **Fill in other words from page 45.**

a) In ____________________, methods of physics and mathematics are used to solve problems in the study of living organisms.

b) In _______________ research, new treatments such as medications or surgical techniques are developed.

c) The structure of DNA was discovered in 1953, which marked the beginning of research into _______________ information.

d) ____________________ food, also called GM food, is produced by applying specific changes to organisms.

6 Complete the sentences with these words.

stomach birth marrow vomit liver

breath brain dehydrated organ genes

synthetic in-vitro fertilisation physical

a) Bones have a soft centre, called ...., where blood cells are produced.

b) In a transplantation an .... is either moved from one body to another, or from a donor site to a patient's body.

c) Drinking too much alcohol damages your ....

d) If you eat too much, your .... may hurt.

e) People with food poisoning often have to ....

f) Does talent lie all in the .... ?

g) Try to drink at least two litres of water every day because being .... can cause headaches and other pains.

h) People with asthma suffer from shortness of ....

i) Mental activities and logical games keep your .... fit.

j) .... exercise enhances your health.

k) Nowadays a lot of health-conscious people refuse to take .... medications if possible and rather take homoeopathic medicines.

l) .... is often the last hope for childless couples, and it has resulted in the .... of over one million babies.

7 **Word families: Write down the corresponding adjectives.**

Noun	Adjective
religion	
Jew	
Muslim	
Koran	
equality	

Noun	Adjective
ethics	
freedom	
tolerance	
virtue	

8 **Match the expressions on the left with the correct German translations. Try to guess if you are not sure.**

1. the will of God
2. freedom of speech
3. blows of fate
4. a deadly disease
5. ethical code
6. gender equality
7. divine justice

a) *Wehen des Schicksals*
b) *Ethikunterricht*
c) *freies Sprechen*
d) *Gleichberechtigung der Geschlechter*
e) *der Wille Gottes*
f) *göttliche Gerechtigkeit*
g) *freie Meinungsäußerung*
h) *eine tödliche Krankheit*
i) *Moralkodex*
j) *kirchliche Justiz*
k) *göttliche Weisheit*
l) *ethnische Herkunft*
m) *Schicksalsschläge*
n) *genetische Übereinstimmung*

1. 2. 3. 4. 5. 6. 7.

Unit 8

Time-out

Tourism		
tourism	Tourismus	→ tourist
catalogue	Katalog	a book with a list of things you can buy
travel	das Reisen	→ traveller → to travel
destination	Ziel, Reiseziel	place to which you are going
faraway	fern, weit entfernt	↔ near, close
booking	Buchung, Reservierung	→ to book
airline	Fluggesellschaft	a company that owns planes and organizes air travel
to depart	abfliegen, abfahren	→ departure
overnight	über Nacht	e.g. an overnight flight
to hire	mieten	= to rent
resort	Ferienort, Badeort	a popular place to go on holiday
attraction	Attraktion, Anziehungspunkt	→ to attract → attractive
sightseeing	Besichtigungstour	looking at tourist attractions
guide	Führer(in)	→ to guide
fascinating	faszinierend	→ fascination → to fascinate
surroundings	Umgebung	the world around us
adventure	Abenteuer	→ adventurer → adventurous
infrastructure	Infrastruktur	the system of a country with regard to transport, energy supply, communication etc.
accessible	zugänglich, befahrbar	→ access
entertainment	Unterhaltung	→ to entertain

= synonym ↔ opposite → word family

Online Link
800037-0008

Nature and environment		
forest	Wald	an area covered with trees, usually larger than a wood
barrier reef	der Küste vorgelagertes Riff	e.g. The Great Barrier Reef is near the coast of Australia.
volcano, *pl.* volcanoes	Vulkan	→ volcanic
thermal	Thermal-, Wärme-	producing or caused by heat
spring	Quelle, Brunnen	water coming from the earth
alive	lebendig	→ life → to live
untouched	unberührt, unversehrt	→ touch → to touch
peaceful	friedlich	→ peace
˙region	Region	→ regional
˙survival	Überleben	→ survivor → to survive
˙planet	Planet	= globe
bioreserve	(Bio-)Reservat	area where nature is protected
˙variety	Vielfalt, Auswahl	a number of different kinds
˙insect	Insekt	an animal with six legs
˙worm	Wurm	e.g. a rainworm
˙root	Wurzel	the part of a plant which grows down into the earth
˙stem	Stamm, Stängel	the central part of a plant
˙leaf, *pl.* leaves	Blatt	one of the green parts of a plant
to preserve	bewahren, erhalten	→ preservation → a preserve
˙naturalist	Naturforscher(in)	→ nature
bin	Mülleimer, Mülltonne	= garbage can *(AE)*
litter	Abfall	= rubbish; garbage, trash *(AE)*
˙carbon footprint	CO_2-Bilanz	emission of carbon dioxide (CO_2)
˙climate	Klima	→ climatic
˙to emit	emittieren, ausstoßen	to give or send out; → emission
˙thunderstorm	Gewitter	a storm with thunder and lightning and heavy rain
˙hurricane	Wirbelsturm, Hurrikan	a strong storm
˙to affect	auswirken, beeinflussen	= to influence

= synonym ↔ opposite → word family

Economy		
˙economic	ökonomisch, wirtschaftlich	→ economy
˙economics	Volkswirtschaftslehre, Wirtschaftswissenschaften	→ economist
sector	Sektor	= part
primary	primär, hauptsächlich, Erst-	= first
secondary	sekundär, Zweit-	→ second
tertiary	tertiär, Dritt-	= third
˙industrial	industriell	→ industry
˙budget	Haushalt, Etat	→ to budget → budgetary
˙investor	Kapitalanleger, Investor	→ investment
˙transaction	Übertragung, Transaktion, Geschäft	an item of business
to establish	aufbauen, (be)gründen	→ establishment
˙to finance	finanzieren	→ finance (e.g. public finance)
˙to thrive	Erfolg haben, gedeihen, blühen	e.g. A thriving business can bring a lot of money into a town.
extraction	Gewinnung, Förderung, Entnahme	taking raw materials out of the ground; → to extract
mining	Bergbau	→ (coal) mine → miner → to mine
˙retailing	Einzelhandel	→ retailer → retail *(adj.)*
˙wholesaler	Großhändler, -handel	→ wholesale *(adj.)*
˙to found	gründen	= to establish
˙branch	Zweigstelle, Niederlassung	e.g. a branch of a global company
˙consolidation	Konsolidierung, Zusammenlegung	→ to consolidate
˙inflation	Inflation	→ inflationary
˙corruption	Korruption, Bestechlichkeit	→ corrupt
˙bankrupt	bankrott, insolvent	→ bankruptcy

= synonym ↔ opposite → word family

Sports		
sporting	sportlich, Sport-	→ sport
jet-skiing	Wassermotorrad fahren	going by jet-ski
paragliding	Gleitschirm fahren	a special way of flying
to hike	wandern	→ hiking → hiker
motorboat	Motorboot	a boat with an engine or a motor
to float	mit dem Floß fahren, treiben, gleiten	to move on a river; → float
˙cycling	Radfahren	→ to cycle
˙ice hockey	Eishockey	a game played on ice with long sticks and a disc called a puck
˙aerobics	Aerobic	special exercises, usually performed to music
˙Pilates	Pilates	an exercise programme
˙ballroom dancing	Gesellschaftstanz	a formal kind of dancing
˙health club	Fitnesscenter	→ health → healthy
˙to get into shape	in Form bringen	to get fit

Exercises

1 What do you call the people described here?

A person who …

a) almost died but continues to live: ....

b) visits a place for pleasure, usually on holiday: ....

c) goes to other places, either for pleasure or on business: ....

d) goes for long walks in the countryside for pleasure: ....

e) enjoys exciting or dangerous experiences: ....

f) leads you through a place and gives you information: ....

2 Find the words on pages 51 and 52 that correspond with the definitions.

a) A mountain which sometimes emits hot material: ....

b) Not changed or damaged by anything: ....

c) A word used to describe places that you can reach easily: ....

d) Quiet and calm: ....

e) To leave from: ....

f) A container for litter: ....

g) The systems a country needs in order to work effectively: ....

h) An area covered with trees: ....

i) A line of rocks in the water near a coast: ....

j) Not dead: ....

k) An arrangement that you make before you go on holiday: ....

3 Complete the sentences.

a) The United States is divided into five r... g... ... ...s: the Northeast, the Southeast, the Midwest, the Southwest and the West.

b) When we went to the US last year, we h... ...ed a car and tr... ... e... ... ...d across the country.

c) We saw many tourist a... ... r... ... t... ... ...s.

d) In the Rocky Mountains we got into a wild summer th... ... ... st... ...m with lightning every second and extremely heavy rain.

e) At the same time a h... ... ... i... ... ...e swept across the southern coast.

4 Read the text and work out the anagrams. Write down the correct words below. Then add the German translations.

My parents and I love to (1) VALRET. When we plan our summer holidays we always spend many hours studying (2) EGOLACUSTA and discussing which (3) NINITEDASOT is the most (4) VATICRETAT. Dad would love to go (5) AWARFYA places such as China or New Zealand, but Mum hates long journeys, especially (6) NIGVROTEH flights. So we usually go to southern Europe. Last summer we went to a beautiful (7) TERORS in Spain. You could do so many things there: relax on the beach, do (8) TOGIRPSN activities, or go for (9) GEGISTSIHEN tours. We visited Jerez and Cadiz, which are (10) SAGNIFITCAN places.

(1) ....

(2) ....

(3) ....

(4) ....

(5) ....

(6) ....

(7) ....

(8) ....

(9) ....

(10) ....

5 Mark the word in each row that does not go with the others. Explain your choice.

a) carbon footprint – climate – naturalist – litter ....

b) airline – resort – surroundings – planet ....

c) attractive – sightseeing – fascinating – popular ....

d) root – stem – leaf – insect ....

e) tourism – faraway – adventure – entertainment ....

f) worm – untouched – regional – natural ....

6 Complete the sentences with these words.

preserve | survival | carbon footprint | Springs | thermal | affect | extraction | bioreserves

a) ______ are home to a large number of wild animals.

b) Hot ______ National Park in Arkansas features 62° ______ waters.

c) If you want to ______ nature, avoid producing too much rubbish.

d) You can find different calculators on the Internet to estimate your ______ ______ and see how much CO_2 your lifestyle creates each year.

e) Vehicle emissions ______ human health and the environment.

f) Accidents in oil ______ can cause severe pollution.

g) A number of leading scientists say that the ______ of our planet depends on our ability to tackle the problems of climate change.

7 Word families: Write down the corresponding nouns or adjectives. Then use a dictionary to add the German translation of each word.

Noun	**Adjective**
corruption – *Korruption, Bestechlichkeit*	
	economic –
budget –	
	bankrupt –
industry –	
	retail –
wholesaler –	
	inflationary –

8 Match the sentence parts.

1. The economy includes
2. The primary sector
3. The secondary sector
4. The tertiary sector
5. An investor
6. Mining is
7. A branch
8. A thriving business
9. In a transaction
10. Financing something
11. If you establish a firm
12. Consolidation

a) deals with the production of goods.
b) the extraction of coal or metals from the ground.
c) means joining things together, for example companies.
d) means providing money for it.
e) involves the extraction and production of raw materials.
f) you found it.
g) something is sold or money is exchanged.
h) puts money into something in order to make a profit.
i) several sectors.
j) has to do with services to consumers and businesses.
k) is a successful business.
l) is a local office or shop that belongs to a large company.

1.	2.	3.	4.	5.	6.	7.	8.	9.	10.	11.	12.

9 Find 11 sports words in this grid. Write them down below. → ← ↓ ↑

G	O	Z	V	E	L	G	N	I	I	K	S	T	E	J	S	C	I	S	N
N	R	F	U	X	O	R	C	W	L	V	A	S	G	E	W	P	Y	E	L
I	B	L	M	O	T	O	R	B	O	A	T	N	R	B	U	N	H	T	H
L	Y	O	N	B	I	B	U	L	C	H	T	L	A	E	H	X	W	A	I
C	L	A	A	E	R	O	B	I	C	S	Y	X	O	R	G	V	U	L	K
Y	W	T	G	N	I	C	N	A	D	M	O	O	R	L	L	A	B	I	I
C	U	N	Y	E	K	C	O	H	E	C	I	V	N	I	H	F	Z	P	N
P	A	R	A	G	L	I	D	I	N	G	R	U	B	X	O	C	Y	L	G

Unit 9

The world is getting smaller

Global trade		
globalisation	Globalisierung	→ global → to globalise
chance	Chance	e.g. Does globalisation offer chances to poorer countries?
risk	Risiko	→ to risk
standard	Standard, Norm, Maßstab	e.g. ethical standards, fair trade standards; → to standardize
industrialized	industrialisiert	industrialized countries ↔ developing countries
· developing world	Entwicklungsländer	Most people in the developing world are poor.
manufacturer	Hersteller	→ manufacturing → to manufacture
merchant	Händler, Kaufmann, Handelsmann	a person who trades products in large amounts
· trader	Händler(in)	→ trade → to trade
to make money	Geld verdienen	to earn a lot of money, to make a profit
logistics	Logistik, Versorgung	having to do with the transportation of goods; → logistic, logistical
guideline	Richtlinie	official advice or rule
to eliminate	beseitigen, entfernen, eliminieren	= to cancel; → elimination
option	Möglichkeit, Alternative	= possibility; → optional
· foreigner	Ausländer(in)	→ foreign

= synonym ↔ opposite → word family

Online Link
800037-0009

Different cultures		
ethnic	ethnisch	An ethnic group shares the same culture, religion, language etc.
authentic	authentisch	= real → authenticity
original	original, ursprünglich, unbearbeitet	→ origin
native	eingeboren, einheimisch	→ native
racial	Rassen-	→ race
diverse	unterschiedlich, vielfältig, verschieden	= different; → diversity
mixture	Mischung	→ to mix
multicultural	multikulturell	→ multiculturalism
Asian	asiatisch	→ Asia
European	europäisch	→ Europe
North/South American	nord-/südamerikanisch	→ North/South America
African	afrikanisch	→ Africa
Australian	australisch	→ Australia

Exercises

1 Word families: Fill in the corresponding words.

Noun	Verb
trader	
	to standardize
risk	
	to mix
manufacturing	
	to eliminate
globalisation	

Noun	Adjective
origin	
	logistical
authenticity	
	diverse
race	
	foreign
option	

= synonym ↔ opposite → word family

2 **What do these words mean? Tick the right answer.**

standard:
a) An opinion you want to defend ☐
b) A rule, often a moral rule, according to which people should act ☐
c) A person's position in a group or in an organization ☐

logistics:
a) thinking and explaining reasons ☐
b) designs or symbols used by companies ☐
c) transporting and delivering goods ☐

native:
a) A person who was born in a particular place ☐
b) A country that is considered as a group of people with the same language and traditions ☐
c) A person who is very good at something without having to learn it ☐

manufacturing:
a) The activity of selling products by advertising them ☐
b) Trading products ☐
c) The business of producing large quantities of products, often from raw materials ☐

diversity:
a) A difference in opinion ☐
b) The condition of being different, for example among a range of people ☐
c) The condition of groups of people who are opposed to each other ☐

elimination:
a) Removing or getting rid of a person or a thing ☐
b) Becoming longer ☐
c) Avoiding a person or a thing ☐

3 **Complete the sentences.**

a) A merchant is a person who ....

b) A foreigner is a person who ....

c) A trader is a person who ....

4 **Write down the names of the continents and the corresponding adjectives.**

Continent	Adjective

5 **Complete the words.**

a) A lot of people think that g……b……l……n has offered the d……p…… world better ……an…… .

b) For example, China is nowadays among the top m……f……t……g countries in the world, and India is m……ing m……n…… in the services sector.

c) New forms of l……g……s have been developed in order to manage international trade.

d) Economic cooperation between countries all over the world has also brought about more e……n……c and cultural d……ty.

e) Thus you can find a m……c……al m……t…… of people in all the large European and American cities.

f) However, critics say that the g……l economy puts poorer countries at r…… of increasing income inequality and makes them dependent on i……d……r……ed countries.

g) Quite a lot of people in poor countries have to work under difficult conditions and they feel exploited by fo……n……s.

h) The Organisation for Economic Co-operation and Development (OECD) points out that human rights, including labour rights, are more important than tr…… rules, and it has therefore issued g……l……es for multinational companies.

Unit 10

International politics

State and government		
democracy	Demokratie	→ democratic
constitution	Verfassung	→ constitutional
unconstitutional	verfassungswidrig	↔ constitutional
president	Präsident	→ presidential
federal	Bundes-	→ federation
parliament	Parlament	→ parliamentary
to make up (s.th.)	etwas bilden, zusammenstellen	e.g. The party makes up over fifty percent of the parliament.
separation of powers	Gewaltenteilung	one of the main principles of democratic states
checks and balances	gegenseitige Kontrolle, Gewaltenteilung	an important part of the US system of government
legislative	legislativ, gesetzgebend	→ legislation
executive	exekutiv, ausführend	The executive branch in politics usually is the government.
judiciary	Judikative, Justizgewalt, Gerichtswesen	→ judicial
Supreme Court	Oberstes Bundesgericht	the highest court in the USA
concentration	Ansammlung, Verdichtung, Konzentration	→ to concentrate
Congress	Kongress (Parlament in den USA)	→ congressional
bill	Gesetzesvorlage	a suggestion for a new law
appointment	Berufung	choosing a person for a position; → to appoint
bureaucracy	Bürokratie	→ bureaucratic

= synonym ↔ opposite → word family

Online Link
800037-0010

The political process		
voter	Wähler(in)	→ to vote
to register	(sich) registrieren, einschreiben, anmelden	e.g. to register to vote; → a register
delegate	Delegierte(r), Abgeordnete(r), Bevollmächtigte(r)	→ to delegate
to represent	repräsentieren, vertreten	= to stand for, to act in place of
majority	Mehrheit	↔ minority
to limit	begrenzen	→ limit; e.g. to limit power
indirect	indirekt, mittelbar	↔ direct; e.g. indirect elections
to function	funktionieren	= to work; → function
to pass	(ein Gesetz) verabschieden	to agree on a law
veto	Veto, Einspruchsrecht, Einspruch	→ to veto ↔ approval
to reverse	umkehren	to change back; → reversal
to nominate	ernennen, nominieren, aufstellen	→ nomination
to approve	anerkennen, bestätigen, zustimmen	→ approval
to permit	erlauben, zulassen, genehmigen	= to allow → permission
to declare	erklären	e.g. to declare war; → declaration
to by-pass	umgehen, überbrücken	To by-pass a law is to break it.
referendum	Referendum, Abstimmung, Volksbefragung	a direct vote in which citizens say "yes" or "no" to a special issue
hostile	feindlich	→ hostility ↔ friendly
opponent	Gegner(in)	↔ supporter → opposition → to oppose → opposite
commissioner	Beauftragte(r), Bevollmächtigte(r)	a person who acts officially for his/her government
to orientate	orientieren, ausrichten	→ orientation
to implement	ausführen, verwirklichen, realisieren	= to carry out, to fulfil; → implementation

= synonym ↔ opposite → word family

International politics		
peacekeeping	Friedenserhaltung, Friedensbewahrung	making sure that a war does not break out
operation	Operation, Handlung	= act, action, activity
commander-in-chief	Oberbefehlshaber	the top leader of the military
leader	Führer(in)	→ to lead
armed forces	Militär, Streitkräfte	airforce, army and navy
treaty	Vertrag	an official agreement between countries or nations
international	international	concerning two or more countries
intergovernmental	zwischenstaatlich, international	= international
enlargement	Vergrößerung, Erweiterung, Erhöhung	e.g. the enlargement of the EU; → to enlarge
continent	Kontinent, Erdteil	e.g. Europe is a continent.
stable	stabil	↔ unstable; → stability
countryman	Landsmann	s.o. who comes from your country
potential	potenziell, eventuell	= possible → potential
accession	Beitritt, Einwilligung, Zuwachs	the point at which a country becomes a member of an organization
criterion, *pl.* criteria	Kriterium, Kriterien	= standard
ally	Alliierte(r), Verbündete(r)	= partner, friend
to disappear	verschwinden	→ disappearance
to afford	sich leisten	to be able to buy or do s.th.
European Monetary Union	Europäische Wirtschafts- und Währungsunion	*(short form)* = EMU
institution	Institution, Einrichtung	e.g. The European Commission is an institution of the EU.
council	Gremium, Rat	= committee
European Court of Justice	Europäischer Gerichtshof	the highest court in the EU

= synonym ↔ opposite → word family

Humanitarian aid		
United Nations	Vereinte Nationen	*(short form)* = UN
humanitarian	humanitär, menschenfreundlich	→ humanity → human
· aid	Hilfe	= help; → to aid
to prevent s.th. from happening/s.o. from doing s.th.	verhindern	e.g. to prevent diseases from breaking out; → prevention
non-governmental	nichtregierungs-, nichtstaatlich	non-governmental organization = NGO
ration	Zuteilung, Ration	a limited amount; → to ration
· to escape (from)	flüchten (vor)	→ escape
to flee, fled, fled	fliehen	= to escape, to run away
condition	Zustand, Situation	e.g. poor living conditions
illiterate	des Lesens und Schreibens unkundig	→ literate
desperate	verzweifelt, aussichtslos	→ despair → to despair
to persecute	verfolgen	→ persecution → persecutor
· slum	Slum, Elendsviertel	poor area of a town
· belongings	Habseligkeiten, Eigentum	→ to belong
refuge	Asyl, Zufluchtsstätte	a place where you can go if you are in danger; → refugee
· migration	Migration, Abwanderung, Umzug	→ migrant → to migrate ↔ immigration
· tragedy	Tragödie	→ tragic
slave	Sklave/Sklavin	→ slavery
short-term	kurzfristig, befristet, kurzzeitig	↔ long-term; e.g. short-term projects
committee	Komitee, Ausschuss, Gremium	e.g. The committee decided to help poor children in Africa.
zone	Zone, Gebiet, Bereich	= area; e.g. war zone
to arrange	organisieren, ausmachen	→ arrangement
to carry out	ausführen	= to do s.th., to complete s.th.

= synonym ↔ opposite → word family

Exercises

1 Match the synonyms and write down the pairs.

to represent | to carry out | to flee | zone | to implement | aid | ally | to function | to complete | operation | standard | committee | to fulfil | to escape | help | partner | to stand for | area | to permit | council | to work | action | to allow | criterion

2 Write down the opposites.

hostile ↔ ....

supporter ↔ ....

majority ↔ ....

stable ↔ ....

direct ↔ ....

long-term ↔ ....

veto ↔ ....

constitutional ↔ ....

3 Complete the sentences.

a) A commissioner is a person who ....

b) A commander-in-chief is ....

c) A countryman is ....

4 **Find six noun-verb pairs in the lists on pages 64 to 66 that have the same forms. Then use a dictionary to add the German translation of each word.**

Noun	Verb

5 **Word families: Fill in the corresponding nouns or adjectives. Then use a dictionary to add the German translation of each word.**

Noun	**Adjective**
legislation – *Legislative, Gesetzgebung*	
	judicial –
federation –	
	bureaucratic –
tragedy –	

6 **Complete the sentences with verbs from this unit.**

a) If a parliament agrees on a bill, it .... the bill.

b) To by-pass a law means to .... it.

c) If you change something back, you .... it.

d) When people say yes to a proposal, they .... it.

e) To .... a person means to choose the person to do a particular job.

f) If you are able to buy something, you can .... it.

g) If you .... an event, you plan and organize it.

7 What do these words mean? Tick the right answer.

delegate:
a) A person who stands in for a leader or manager while he or she is away ☐
b) A person who is voted for and then represents the voters' interests ☐
c) A leader of a political party ☐

to persecute:
a) To accuse a person of committing a crime in a court ☐
b) To continue doing something, even if you have extreme problems ☐
c) To treat people in a cruel or unfair way, especially because of their religion, race or political opinions ☐

illiterate:
a) Not having a formal education ☐
b) Not being able to read and write ☐
c) Knowing nothing about literature ☐

despair:
a) The feeling you have when you have lost all hope ☐
b) The inability to help other people ☐
c) A very difficult situation ☐

hostility:
a) Unfriendly or aggressive behaviour ☐
b) Very friendly behaviour towards guests ☐
c) A feeling of great shock or fear ☐

8 Match the sentence parts.

1. The Supreme Court
2. The separation of powers is
3. Checks and balances
4. When states or communities work together at the international level,
5. EMU
6. The European Court of Justice

a) is a division into three branches: executive, legislative and judicial.
b) is the short form of European Monetary Union.
c) we call this intergovernmental cooperation.
d) is a term used in the American constitution for the separation of powers.
e) is the highest court in the EU.
f) is the highest court in the United States.

1. 2. 3. 4. 5. 6.

9 **Complete the sentences with these words.**

refuge slums migrated conditions humanitarian

prevent rations persecution declarations

a) The United Nations was established after World War II in order to .... further international aggressions and .... of war.

b) The UN undertook its first .... aid operations in Europe.

c) The living .... in urban .... are characterized by poor hygiene and violence.

d) Throughout history, people have .... for a variety of reasons: poverty, religious ...., or lack of political freedom.

e) Turkey has become a .... for people fleeing from Iran.

f) Providing large numbers of refugees with food .... is a logistical challenge.

10 **Make expressions that correspond with the German phrases.**

non-governmental • safety • refugee • desperate • personal • short-term • peacekeeping • armed

situation • measures • forces • zone • mission • belongings • organization • camp

.... – *Friedensmission*

.... – *verzweifelte Lage*

.... – *Streitkräfte*

.... – *Flüchtlingslager*

.... – *Nichtregierungsorganisation*

.... – *persönliche Habe*

.... – *Sicherheitszone*

.... – *kurzfristige Maßnahmen*

11 Translate the clues and write the English words in the crossword.

Across:
- 4 ausrichten
- 5 verschwinden
- 10 Ansammlung
- 12 Vertrag
- 13 ausführend
- 14 Ausschuss

Down:
- 1 Verfassung
- 2 Demokratie
- 3 Volksbefragung
- 6 Beitritt
- 7 Berufung
- 8 Wähler
- 9 Gesetzesvorlage
- 11 Erweiterung

Units 11–14

Cross-cultural communication

Meeting and talking to people		
conversation	Gespräch, Unterhaltung, Konversation	When people talk to each other, they have a conversation.
· dialogue *(BE)*	Dialog, Gespräch	dialog *(AE)*
to shake, shook, shaken	schütteln	e.g. to shake hands
pleased	erfreut	= happy, glad; e.g. Pleased to meet you.
informal	informell	→ informality; ↔ formal
response	Reaktion, Antwort	= reaction, answer; → to respond
face-to-face	persönlich, von Angesicht zu Angesicht	relating to a situation in which you see s.o. you are talking to
to be in touch	in Verbindung stehen, in Kontakt bleiben	e.g. We'll be in touch.
intense	angestrengt, intensiv	→ intensity
· to maintain	behaupten	to express s.th. firmly
to inquire	sich erkundigen, fragen	→ inquiry
to give s.o. a buzz	jdn. anrufen	*(colloquial)* = to call s.o.
· caller	Anrufer(in)	→ to call
to phone	anrufen, telefonieren	= to call
incoming	eingehend	e.g. incoming calls
· busy	besetzt, belegt	e.g. The line is busy right now.
to catch s.th.	etwas akustisch verstehen	to hear and understand s.th.
inconvenience	Unannehmlichkeit, Belästigung	e.g. Sorry for the inconvenience; → inconvenient
to cut a long story short	langer Rede kurzer Sinn	to say it briefly

= synonym ↔ opposite → word family

Online Link
800037-0011

Writing letters and e-mails		
draft	Entwurf, Skizze	→ draftsman → to draft
reference	Referenz, Bezug	a letter that is written by s.o. who knows you to say you are suitable for a job; or: s.th. you refer to for information
· to refer (to)	sich beziehen auf	→ reference
· with reference to	betreffend, bezüglich	→ reference → to refer (to)
salutation	Begrüßung, Anrede	You always start a letter with a salutation.
request	Nachfrage, Anfrage	→ to request
apology	Entschuldigung	→ to apologize
to appreciate	schätzen	→ appreciation
to be delighted	glücklich sein, sehr zufrieden sein	to be very happy
· thankful	dankbar	→ thanks → to thank
· to confirm	bestätigen, bestärken	→ confirmation
sincerely	Mit freundlichen Grüßen	Yours sincerely = Yours faithfully
complimentary close	Grußformel	Yours …; Yours sincerely …; Sincerely …; Kind regards … are examples of complimentary closes.
attachment	Anhang, Anbringung	→ to attach
dot	Punkt	= full stop; e.g. A sentence ends with a dot.
· colloquial	umgangssprachlich	referring to informal language
· bracket	Klammer	These are brackets: ( ).
· to recommend	empfehlen	→ recommendation
· accommodation	Unterbringung	→ to accommodate
to charge	in Rechnung stellen, berechnen	→ charge
reduction	Reduzierung	→ to reduce
rate	Rate, Preis	amount of money you pay for s.th.

= synonym ↔ opposite → word family

Different cultures		
culture	Kultur	→ cultural
· multi-ethnic	multiethnisch	with people from different ethnic groups; → ethnicity
· inter-racial	zwischen Rassen, verschiedenen Rassen gemeinsam	→ race
· relations	Verhältnis, Beziehung	e.g. relations between countries
overseas	Übersee-, in Übersee	referring to foreign countries
· unique	einzigartig	→ uniqueness
· to identify	identifizieren, erkennen	→ identification → identifiable
queue	Warteschlange	→ to queue
Brit *(informal)*	Brite	a person who comes from Britain
Aussie *(informal)*	Australier(in)	= Australian
dress code	Kleiderordnung	what you have to wear
stranger	Fremde(r)	a person you don't know
· cosmopolitan atmosphere	weltoffene Atmosphäre	→ a cosmopolitan

Exercises

1 Word families: Fill in the corresponding nouns or verbs.

Noun	Verb
draft	
	to attach
reference	
	to appreciate
reduction	
	to accommodate
identification	
	to respond

Noun	Verb
apology	
	to inquire
queue	
	to confirm
caller	
	to recommend
request	
	to identify

= synonym ↔ opposite → word family

2 Choose verbs from exercise 1 to complete these sentences.

If you …

a) … notice the positive characteristics of something, you ________ it.

b) … send a file with an e-mail, you ________ it.

c) … write down the first rough version of a text, you ________ it.

d) … very politely ask someone to do something, you ________ this.

e) … say that you are sorry for something you have said or done, you ________.

f) … recognize a person and can say who he or she is, you ________ the person.

g) … lower the price of a product, you ________ it.

h) … give someone a buzz, you ________ the person.

3 Word families: Fill in the corresponding nouns or adjectives.

Noun	Adjective
inconvenience	
	ethnic
culture	

Noun	Adjective
uniqueness	
	intense
informality	

4 Choose words from exercise 3 to complete these sentences.

a) You can wear casual clothes to ________ meetings.

b) A thing that is ________ is the only thing of a kind.

c) Something that does not suit you or causes you trouble is an ________.

d) Something that is very strong or very great is ________.

e) The ________ diversity across industrialized countries will increase in the next few decades.

5 You are doing a work placement. Write down what you say in the following situations.

a) Sie sagen einer Person, dass Sie sich freuen, sie kennen zu lernen.

....

b) Sie fassen Ihre bisherigen Ausführungen zusammen und leiten dies mit „langer Rede kurzer Sinn" ein.

....

c) Sie entschuldigen sich bei Ihrem Gesprächspartner für eine Unannehmlichkeit.

....

d) Sie sagen jemandem zum Abschluss eines Gesprächs, dass Sie in Kontakt bleiben.

....

e) Sie haben bei einem Telefongespräch etwas akustisch nicht verstanden.

....

f) Sie sagen einem Anrufer, der verbunden werden möchte, dass alle Telefonleitungen besetzt sind.

....

6 Complete the sentences with words from page 72.

a) If you .... that you don't know a person, you say this again and again, especially if other people don't believe you.

b) Employers say that .... communication is extremely important for keeping staff up-to-date.

c) Routine .... between employers and employees are necessary for a good work atmosphere.

d) Call centre agents often have to answer hundreds of .... phone calls each day.

7 Read the clues and complete the grid.

1 A letter always starts with a …
2 You write the … line between the date and number 1
3 You end a letter with a …
4 If you are grateful to a person, you … them.
5 In a formal letter you use this word to express that you are very happy about something.
6 You often put additional information in …, for example dates and time spans.
7 An example of number 3

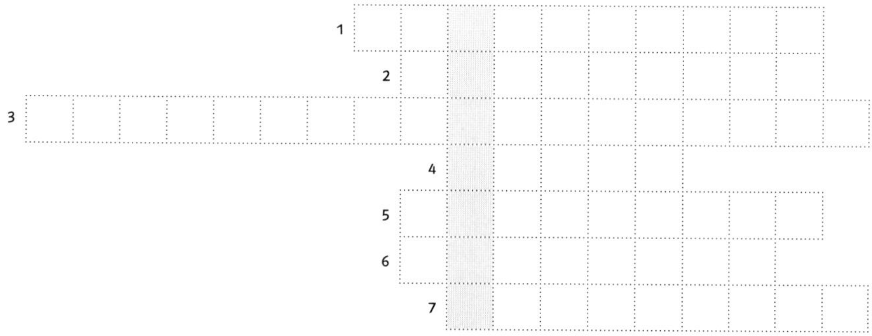

The solution can have two meanings. How can you translate the word?

8 Match the sentence parts.

1. When you read out the URL *magic.com*,
2. Hotels often offer
3. They should not charge you
4. An accommodation
5. If you make a price inquiry,
6. A draftsman

a) creates technical drawings.
b) special weekend rates.
c) you ask how much something will cost.
d) is a place of temporary residence.
e) you say "magic dot com".
f) for Internet access.

1. 2. 3. 4. 5. 6.

9 Use these words to complete the sentences.

informal	colloquial	inter-racial	shake
overseas	relations	dress code	conversations
strangers	cosmopolitan	identifiable	intense

a) New York has a .... atmosphere because you can meet people from many different parts of the world who either live there or are visitors from ....

b) .... marriages are marriages between people from different ethnic groups.

c) In the last few decades, religious and cultural diversity have become important factors in international ....

d) You can't wear jeans and T-shirts if you are doing a work placement in Britain or the United States, so find out about the .... before you start.

e) Keep in mind that British people don't .... hands as often as Germans.

f) If you don't conform to the different habits when staying in another country, you are easily .... as a foreigner.

g) You shouldn't use .... expressions in business .... , but you can of course use a few in .... situations.

h) Never become too emotional or .... when making small talk to ....

Units 1–20

Social topics

Jobs		
carer	Betreuer(in), Pfleger(in)	→ care → to care
childminder	Tagesmutter	woman who looks after other people's children
nanny	Kindermädchen	a woman whose job is to take care of a family's children
nursery school teacher	Erzieher(in)	→ nursery school
child carer	Erzieher(in), Kinderbetreuer(in)	a person who looks after other people's children
family doctor	Hausarzt, -ärztin	doctor that families go to when they are sick
teaching assistant	Lehrkraft, die im Unterricht unterstützt	→ assistance → to assist
communicator	Sprecher(in)	→ communication → to communicate
supervisor	Betreuer(in)	→ supervision → to supervise
social worker	Sozialarbeiter(in)	→ social work
physiotherapist	Physiotherapeut(in)	→ physiotherapy
nutritionist	Ernährungsberater(in)	→ nutrition
addictions counsellor	Suchttherapeut(in)	→ addiction → addict → addicted (to)
probation assistant	Bewährungshelfer(in)	person who helps people who have committed a crime for a year or two
warden	Aufsicht, Wärter(in), Betreuer(in)	person who is responsible for a group of people
official	Amtsperson, Beamter/Beamtin	person working for the state

= synonym ↔ opposite → word family

Online Link
800037-0015

Health problems and disabilities		
disease	Krankheit	= illness
dementia	Demenz, Verwirrtheit	serious illness which affects one's brain and memory
overweight	übergewichtig	→ weight → to weigh
to be disabled	behindert sein	= to be handicapped; → disability
blind	blind	→ blindness
deaf	gehörlos, taub	→ deafness
hard of hearing	schwerhörig	not able to hear well
hearing loss	Gehörschädigung, Gehörverlust	development where s.o. loses the ability to hear
sign language	Gebärdensprache	a way of communicating using hand signals instead of words
injured	verletzt	= hurt; → injury
wheelchair	Rollstuhl	a chair with wheels that people use who are not able to walk
multiple sclerosis	Multiple Sklerose	serious illness which makes it difficult for people to move, speak and see
arthritis	Arthritis, Gelenkentzündung	painful condition affecting the joints
joint	Gelenke	the connection of two bones in your body
diabetes	Diabetes, Zuckerkrankheit	→ diabetic
cholera	Cholera	a serious infection of the bowels caused by infected water
infection	Infektion, Ansteckung	→ to infect → infectious
bacteria, *sing.* bacterium	Bakterien	→ bacterial
to suffer	leiden	to experience pain; → suffering
depression	Depression, Niedergeschlagenheit	→ depressed
widespread	(weit)verbreitet	happening or existing in many places

= synonym ↔ opposite → word family

Medicine and healthcare		
medical	medizinisch	→ medicine
healthcare	Gesundheitswesen, medizinische Versorgung	all the services provided by a country for ill people
clinic	Klinik	= hospital
ward	Station, Abteilung	one part of a hospital
unit	Abteilung, Station	= ward; department at a hospital
maternity ward	Entbindungsstation	ward where women have babies
gynecology	Gynäkologie, Frauenheilkunde	→ gynecologist
geriatric	geriatrisch	relating to old people; e.g. geriatric ward
Accident & Emergency unit	Notaufnahme, Notfallstation	the part of a hospital to which people are taken who have had serious accidents
patient	Patient(in)	person who receives medical treatment
patient-centred	mit dem Patienten im Mittelpunkt	where the sick person comes first
outpatients	Ambulanz	part of a hospital where you receive treatment but do not stay for the night
radiologist	Radiologe/Radiologin	→ radiology
specialist	Spezialist(in)	→ to specialize
to recover	sich erholen	to get better after an illness or a shock; → recovery
new-born	neu geboren	→ to bear, bore, born → birth
home	Heim	place where people live and are looked after
secure	sicher, geschützt	refers to a place that you cannot easily leave; → security
chemist's *(BE)*	Apotheke	drugstore *(AE)*; e.g. Please take this prescription to the chemist's.

= synonym ↔ opposite → word family

Medical and psychological treatment		
treatment	Behandlung	→ to treat
to cure	heilen	→ cure
diagnosis	Diagnose	→ to diagnose
bandage	Verband	→ to bandage
pill	Pille, Tablette	one form of medicine
antibiotic	Antibiotikum	a medicine that destroys harmful bacteria in the body
bacteria, *sing.* bacterium	Bakterien	→ bacterial
injection	Injektion, Spritze	→ to inject
vaccine	Impfstoff	→ vaccination → to vaccinate
immune	immun, geschützt	safe from a disease; → immunization → immune system
insulin	Insulin	substance in your body which controls the level of sugar in your blood
to operate (on)	operieren	→ operation
surgery	Operation, Chirurgie, (Arzt-)Praxis	→ surgeon → surgical
transplant	Transplantation	e.g. a heart transplant; → to transplant
mechanical heart	Kunstherz	a machine that helps the heart to work
donor	Spender(in)	→ donation → to donate
X-ray	Röntgen, Röntgenbild	→ to X-ray
check-up	Untersuchung, Vorsorgeuntersuchung	examination to make sure that you are healthy
psychology	Psychologie	→ psychologist → psychological
occupational therapy	Beschäftigungstherapie	refers to special work that helps s.o. to manage their disability; → therapist
to cope with	bewältigen	= to manage

= synonym ↔ opposite → word family

Society and social issues		
society	Gesellschaft	→ social
situation	Situation	the present conditions
environment	Umgebung, Umfeld	the people and things around you
community	Gemeinde, Gemeinschaft	e.g. Our village is a small community.
norm	Norm, Regel	a way of behaving that people expect from you; → normal
tradition	Tradition	→ traditional
conventional	konventionell, normal	= normal, typical; → convention
poverty	Armut	→ poor
divide	Kluft, Trennlinie, Grenze	→ division → to divide
migration	Migration	→ migrant → to migrate
benefit	Sozialhilfe, Rente	→ to benefit
welfare	Sozialhilfe, Wohlfahrt	money provided by the state to people who have no job
homelessness	Obdachlosigkeit	not having a home; → homeless
illiteracy	Analphabetismus	→ illiterate
prejudice	Vorurteil	→ prejudiced
discrimination	Diskriminierung	to discriminate (against)
racism	Rassismus	→ racist
binge drinking	Besäufnis, Komasaufen	the consumption of large quantities of alcohol within a short period of time
excessive	maßlos, exzessiv, zu viel	→ excess
deprived	sozial benachteiligt	→ deprivation
to hang around	herumhängen	to wait and not do very much
failure	Versagen	→ to fail
childcare	Kinderbetreuung	→ child carer
rundown	abgewirtschaftet, verwahrlost	e.g. The building was empty and completely rundown.
derelict	heruntergekommen	in bad condition
focus	Blickpunkt, Mittelpunkt, Fokus	a central point of attention, e.g. focus on childcare

= synonym ↔ opposite → word family

Crime and punishment		
criminal	kriminell, verbrecherisch	→ crime → a criminal
gang	Gang, Bande	group of criminals working together
offence	Straftat	→ offender → to offend
to commit	begehen (Verbrechen)	to do s.th. that is illegal
shoplifting	Ladendiebstahl	stealing things from a shop
drug	Droge	e.g. marihuana, cocaine, heroin
to investigate	ermitteln	→ investigation
to give chase to s.o.	jdn. verfolgen	→ chase → to chase
victim	Opfer	s.o. who has been injured or killed as the result of a crime
warning	Warnung, Verwarnung, Abmahnung	→ to warn
reprimand	Verwarnung, Tadel	→ to reprimand
punishment	Strafe, Bestrafung	→ to punish
guilty	schuldig	e.g. to be guilty of a crime; → guilt
fault	Fehler, Schuld	a mistake s.o. has made
Anti Social Behaviour Order	einstweilige gerichtliche Verfügung wegen antisozialen Verhaltens	An ASBO stops young people from going to particular places or doing particular things.
client	betreute(r) Jugendliche(r)	s.o. who uses a service that provides help or care
conviction	Verurteilung	finding s.o. guilty of a crime; → convict → to convict
judgement	Urteil, Beurteilung	→ judge → to judge
severe	streng, ernst	= strict, serious
authority	Behörde, Autorität	an organisation or public service that looks after a certain area
to reintegrate	reintegrieren	e.g. to reintegrate criminals into society; → reintegration

= synonym ↔ opposite → word family

Conflicts and violence		
violence	Gewalt	→ violent
abuse	Beschimpfungen, Schimpfwörter; Missbrauch	→ to abuse
quarrel	Streit, Auseinander-setzung	→ to quarrel
confrontation	Konfrontation, Ausein-andersetzung	→ to confront
to terrorize	terrorisieren	→ terror → terrorist
cruel	grausam	→ cruelty
horrible	schrecklich	= terrible
slap	Schlag	a sharp blow with your hand; → to slap
fatal	tödlich	causing death, deadly
bullying	Mobbing, Schikanieren	being aggressive towards s.o. weaker; → bully → to bully
hand grenade	Handgranate	small bomb that s.o. throws or fires from a gun
gun	Schusswaffe	a type of weapon
at risk	gefährdet	→ risk (of death) → to risk → risky
incident	Vorfall	an event which can be dangerous or criminal
hate	Hass	→ to hate
to defend	verteidigen	→ defence; ↔ to attack
self-defence	Selbstverteidigung, Notwehr	e.g. to hit s.o. in self-defence
dispute	Auseinandersetzung, Streit	= fight
drunken	betrunken	e.g. a drunken person
to deny	abstreiten	to say that s.th. is not true; → denial
to settle	beilegen, begleichen	to put an end to a fight; → settlement

= synonym ↔ opposite → word family

1 What are these people's jobs?

a) Mr Jenkins helps people who have problems moving. He is a …………………… .

b) Mrs Raymond has two children of her own and she also looks after four other children who come to her house in the morning. She is a …………………… .

c) Her sister is a …………………… in a nursery school.

d) Amy Dawson plans food programmes for people with health problems, for example people who are overweight or have allergies. Amy is a …………………… .

e) Jeremy Barton supervises young people who have committed a crime, but have been given the chance to improve their behaviour. He is a …………………… .

f) Gemma Nichols helps people with drug problems. She is an …………………… .

g) Richard Eames works for the city of Birmingham and takes care of at-risk youth in deprived areas. He is a …………………… .

h) Bob Williamson works in a prison. Among his tasks is making sure that the prisoners have food and clothes, get the programmes they need and are secure in the prison. Bob is a …………………… .

2 Complete the descriptions.

a) A nanny is a person who ……………………

b) A teaching assistant is a person who ……………………

c) An official is ……………………

d) A family doctor is ……………………

3 **Word families: Fill in the corresponding nouns and verbs.**

Noun (job or act)	Noun (person)	Verb
supervision		
	carer	
		to communicate
judgement		
	offender	
terror		
	bully	

4 **Find 12 words for health problems and disabilities in this grid. Letters may overlap. Write down the words below.** → ← ↓ ↑

A	B	R	T	M	F	A	V	H	W	M	Z	O	Q	K	U	B	C	O	S
K	L	M	U	L	T	I	P	L	E	S	C	L	E	R	O	S	I	S	E
I	I	N	F	E	C	T	I	O	N	Q	G	N	H	P	Q	D	R	S	T
N	N	Z	N	O	U	N	C	F	H	A	R	E	L	O	H	C	F	E	E
J	D	B	F	R	O	E	A	D	D	I	C	T	I	O	N	G	M	N	B
U	N	E	Q	U	N	M	S	I	T	I	R	H	T	R	A	R	Z	F	A
R	E	W	U	M	Z	E	P	W	N	C	V	D	M	G	W	U	Q	A	I
Y	S	O	N	P	R	D	C	D	R	N	O	I	S	S	E	R	P	E	D
Q	S	S	O	L	G	N	I	R	A	E	H	Z	P	C	H	M	O	D	T

5 Complete the sentences with words and phrases from page 80. Sometimes you have to use plural forms.

a) People with arthritis suffer from __________ pain and may need a mobility aid, such as a walking stick or a __________.

b) Infections are caused by viruses or by __________.

c) A strict diet can help you if you are __________.

d) People communicating in __________ use their hands when talking.

e) This form of communication is used by most people who are __________, and sometimes also by people who are __________.

f) Hunger, pain, crime and war are __________ causes of __________.

6 Complete the words. You can find all of them on page 81.

a) The aim of p_t_nt-c_nt_d h_l_c_re in hospitals is to provide all patients with top-class tr_t_t – from n_w-b_n babies to the elderly.

b) A r_d_l_g_st is a sp_t who makes X-r_s.

c) If you want to become a nurse in a m_t_rn_ty w_d, you need special training.

d) There are sp_c_l_zed g_n_c_l_gy c_n_cs for women with complex health issues.

e) G_r_tr_c home c_e programmes provide support for older p_t_n_s who don't live in h_m_s but are unable to leave the house in order to see a doctor.

f) People who have had a heart attack must be taken to an A_id_t & E_rg_n_y u_t.

7 Translate the clues and write the English words in the crossword.

Across:
1 Verband
4 Insulin
7 Antibiotikum
10 Spender(in)
13 Spritze
14 Tablette
15 immun
16 Chirurgie
17 Psychologie
19 mechanisches Herz

Down:
2 Apotheke *(AE)*
3 Ambulanz
5 Erholung, Genesung
6 Transplantation
8 operieren
9 Vorsorgeuntersuchung
11 Diagnose
12 Impfstoff
18 Kur

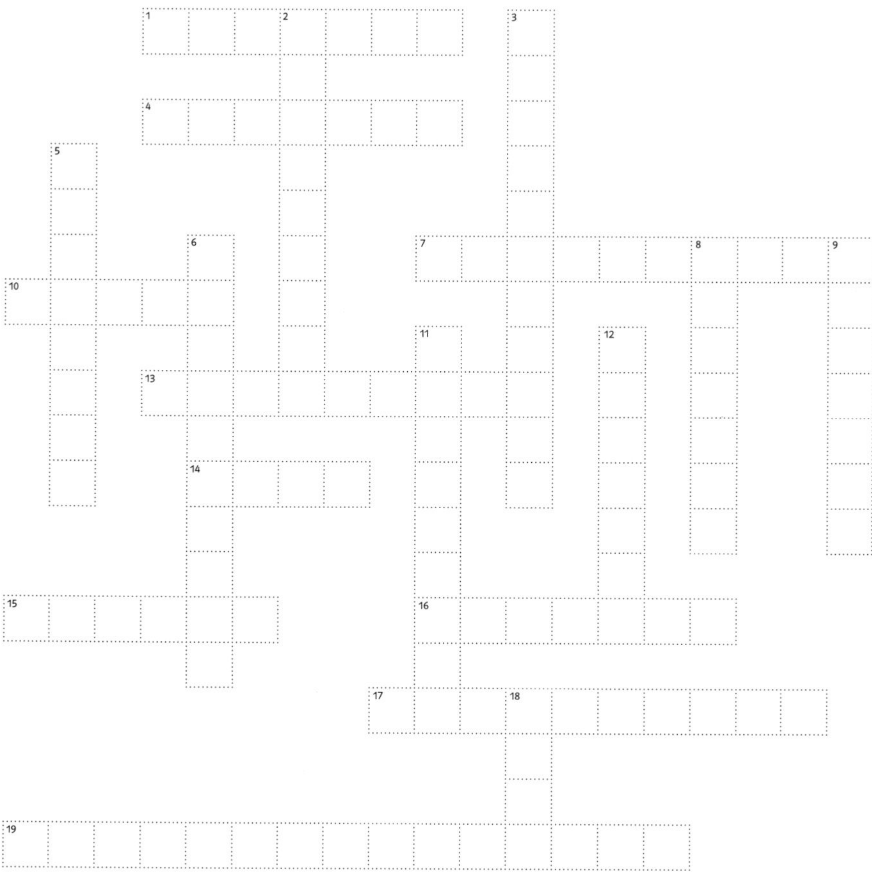

8 **Word families: Fill in the corresponding words.**

Noun	Verb
transplant	
	to chase
donation	
	to divide
X-ray	
	to discriminate (against)
diagnosis	
	to migrate
bandage	
	to benefit
investigation	
	to abuse

Noun	Adjective
medicine	
	secure
bacteria	
	racist
surgery	
	deprived
society	
	illiterate
prejudice	
	excessive
convention	
	homeless

9 **Match the words on the left with the definitions on the right.**

1	tradition	A	all the people living in one place who are regarded as a group
2	failure	B	a way of behaving that people expect from you
3	community	C	disadvantaged in some way
4	poverty	D	not taken care of and therefore in a very bad condition
5	violence	E	something that people in a society have done for a long time
6	rundown	F	a central point of attention
7	focus	G	lack of success
8	deprived	H	hurting or even killing others
9	norm	I	the condition of being poor

1		2		3		4		5		6		7		8		9	

10 **Use these words to complete the sentences.**

fault hang reprimand welfare crime gang
binge drinking situation guilty cope punishment
shoplifting derelict drug environments societies

a) Excessive alcohol consumption, or ……………………,
has become a major concern for western …………………… .

b) According to UK police reports there has been a sharp increase in drink-related
…………………… .

c) Most young people consume alcohol in public drinking ……………………,
such as pubs or bars.

d) …………………… areas are often social hot spots.

e) A lot of people there are dependent on public …………………… .

f) Youngsters who can't find a job after leaving school just …………………… around all day
and try to …………………… with their desolate …………………… .

g) …………………… abuse and …………………… violence are frequent problems in such areas.

h) An Anti-Social Behaviour Order can be issued in response to incidents such as
……………………, prohibiting an offender's return to a shop.

i) A …………………… is a warning given by a police officer to a young
person who is …………………… of a minor offence.

j) Teenagers who admit …………………… for a crime can often avoid severe
…………………… and are given a second chance.

11 **Find the words on pages 84 and 85 that correspond with the definitions.**

a) A person who has been attacked, injured or killed: ....

b) An official agreement that ends a conflict: ....

c) Someone who is being helped by a professional person or an organization: ....

d) Protecting yourself: ....

e) An argument or a disagreement: ....

f) A fight, either verbal or physical: ....

g) Finding a person guilty of a crime: ....

h) Bad words used to insult or attack another person: ....

12 **Write down synonyms.**

horrible – ....

severe – ....

conventional – ....

disability – ....

disease – ....

to cope with – ....

operation – ....

hospital – ....

ward – ....

injured – ....

13 **Mark the word in each row that does not go with the others. Explain your choice.**

a) to punish – to convict – to reprimand – to defend ....

b) hate – cruel – horrible – fatal ....

c) hand grenade – gun – slap – weapon ....

d) incident – cruelty – terrorist – confrontation ....

e) defence – attack – quarrel – abuse ....

14 **Translate these phrases.**

a) *Beschäftigungstherapie für Senioren:* ....

b) *qualifizierte Kinderbetreuung:* ....

c) *örtliche Behörden:* ....

d) *betrunkene Jugendliche:* ....

e) *gesellschaftliche Wiedereingliederung:* ....

f) *soziale Konventionen:* ....

g) *ein Verbrechen begehen:* ....

h) *einen Verbrecher verfolgen:* ....

i) *ein Verbrechen abstreiten:* ....

j) *in Todesgefahr:* ....

k) *einen Schulhofschläger konfrontieren:* ....

l) *gesellschaftliche Kluft:* ....

Key to the exercises

Unit 1: Young people in Europe

1 1 Science 2 project 3 fail 4 leaver 5 presentation 6 Geography 7 essay Solution: college

2 impression – to impress residence – to reside campaigning – to campaign failure – to fail trainee – to train dislike – to dislike replacement – to replace management (or: manager) – to manage practicability – practicable (or: practical) leaver – to leave behaviour – to behave presentation – to present achievement – to achieve studies – to study work (or: worker, workplace) – to work assistant – to assist aid – to aid operative – to operate

3 a) lifestyle b) subculture c) country of origin d) religion e) condition f) under-age g) settle

4 1G 2D 3I 4A 5H 6B 7E 8C 9F

5 citizenship – nationality to monitor – to observe replacement – substitute workmate – colleague

6 (Brendan) National Diploma; further education; placement; nine-to-five job
(Germaine) Health and Social Care; workplace
(Damian) apprenticeship; orders; staff
(Rachel) part-time job; on duty; colleagues; day; sales talks

Unit 2: Working in a social environment

1 a) potential b) ability c) rejection d) essential e) beneficial; relevant; aspects f) equivalent

2 action – to act – active challenge – to challenge – challenging reliability – to rely (on) – reliable creativity – to create – creative requirement – to require – requisite demand – to demand – demanding discipline – to discipline – disciplined qualification – to qualify (for) – qualified suitability – to suit – suitable

3 challenge: b) fluency: a) self-confidence: b) requirement: b) reputation: c)

4 1 responsibility 2 agency 3 vacancy 4 rejection 5 curriculum vitae 6 enclosed 7 advert 8 eagerness 9 application 10 long-term 11 requisite 12 talented 13 candidate 14 qualified 15 active

A	E	A	G	E	R	N	E	S	S	N	U	H	K	Y	M	U	E	Y
P	B	E	A	T	I	V	M	U	L	U	C	I	R	R	U	C	D	C
P	P	Y	C	T	J	S	M	R	E	T	G	N	O	L	I	W	E	N
L	B	R	A	G	E	N	C	Y	N	Q	E	V	I	T	C	A	S	A
I	S	E	K	E	F	D	R	M	J	E	W	P	F	U	A	D	O	C
C	C	A	N	D	I	D	A	T	E	W	K	U	E	M	J	H	L	A
A	M	R	K	L	Y	G	H	N	O	I	T	C	E	J	E	R	C	V
T	O	D	E	T	N	E	L	A	T	O	B	C	L	W	E	Q	N	F
I	G	Y	Y	T	I	L	I	B	I	S	N	O	P	S	E	R	E	S
O	A	D	V	E	R	T	E	C	Y	Q	U	A	L	I	F	I	E	D
N	P	S	Y	R	L	E	T	I	S	I	U	Q	E	R	E	F	L	D

5 a) trustworthy b) musical c) reliable (or: responsible) d) eager e) talented

Unit 3: Young people as consumers

1 to distribute – distribution to promote – promotion to create – creation to regulate – regulation to delete – deletion to operate – operation

All the nouns end in -ion. When adding the ending to a verb you have to leave out the final -e.

2 purchase – to purchase bid – to bid range – to range target – to target label – to label alert – to alert scam – to scam ban – to ban

3 a) target b) ban c) scam d) alert e) label f) bid g) range h) purchase

4 a) trendy (an adjective, not a noun)
b) operator (a company, not a mobile phone feature)
c) scam (a crime, not a legal measure)
d) auction (a form of selling, not a form of advertising)
e) flyer (a thing, not a person)

5 1 discount 2 must-have 3 consumer 4 payment 5 inexpensive
6 silver 7 fashionable 8 packaging Solution: shopping

6 a) create; promotion b) logo; merchandising c) sponsoring; marketing
d) no-name products; branded products; advertised
e) Billboards; advertisements; slogans f) advertising agencies; based

7 a) features b) credit c) reload d) Telecommunications e) Text messages
f) ringtones; wallpapers g) Instant h) electronic i) battery
j) premium rate number k) Short codes

8 1.d) 2.f) 3.e) 4.a) 5.c) 6.b)

9 a) confirmation b) unique c) on offer d) Advertising agencies
e) Accessories

10 a) persuade b) try ... on c) exchange d) change your mind e) unpack

Unit 4: Living with the media

1 **Across:** 3 data 5 update 6 wireless 8 keypad 9 web 12 button
13 file 14 programming language 15 screen
Down: 1 games console 2 top-level domain 4 instant messaging 7 icon
10 desktop 11 provider

2 browser – to browse click – to click killing – to kill witness – to witness
comment – to comment conclusion – to conclude summary – to summarize
download – to download proposal – to propose report – to report
suggestion – to suggest analysis – to analyze

3 a) comment; pros and cons b) context c) summary d) analysis; point out
e) suggest f) proposal

4 Suggested answers:
a) A judge is a person who decides in court.
b) A murderer is a person who has killed someone.
c) A reporter is a person who informs you about events on the radio or on TV.

5 (1) piracy – *Piraterie* (2) downloaded – *heruntergeladen*
(3) stealing – *Stehlen* (4) illegal – *illegal* (5) observed – *beobachtet*
(6) responsible – *verantwortlich, haftbar* (7) punish – *bestrafen*
(8) courts – *Gerichte* (9) files – *Dateien* (10) prison – *Gefängnis*

Unit 5: Developments in society

1 relationship opportunity motivation interaction function
organization profession feminism salary education
contraception commitment

2 pregnancy – pregnant volunteer – voluntary marriage – married
beauty – beautiful interaction – interactive demographics – demographic
mechanic – mechanical function – functional labour – labour
impotence – impotent engagement – engaged man – male

3 gym – *Turnhalle* – sports hall opportunity – *Gelegenheit, Chance* – chance
single parent – *Alleinerziehende(r)* – lone parent
class time – *Unterrichtszeit* – lessons mark – *Zensur* – grade
corridor – *Flur* – hall (or: hallway)

4 to be pregnant, to be married, to be engaged
to get pregnant, to get married, to get engaged, to get a low wage, to get good marks, to get a high salary
to have a conference, to have a relationship, to have a low wage, to have a high salary, to have an affair
to become pregnant, to become engaged

to become = *werden; bekommen* = to get

5 a) contraception; pregnancies b) condoms c) feminist d) female beauty
e) engaged; marry f) wedding; honeymoon g) single mums h) childcare
i) raising j) grandchildren

6 a) professions b) commitment; unpaid c) mechanical d) labour e) opportunities
f) Shift g) routine; organized h) motivation; commitment; tasks
i) interact; organizational j) conference

7 1 canteen 2 courtyard 3 primary 4 residential 5 certificate
6 comprehensive 7 library 8 GCSE 9 campus 10 exchange
11 coaching 12 secondary 13 special needs Solution: nursery school

Unit 6: Environment and education

1 rainfall biofuel wildlife overfishing countryside seafood
rainforest bioreserve carbohydrate

2 a) overfishing b) countryside c) wildlife d) bioreserve

3 negative ↔ positive complex ↔ easy to save ↔ to waste
increasing ↔ decreasing

4 a) creature b) conservation c) crystal d) exploitation e) recycling
f) algae g) ecology h) desert i) sewage j) improvement

5 a) Ecology b) exploitation c) improvement d) conservation e) recycling

6 a) provide b) run out c) harms d) aims e) identify f) contribute

7 disaster – catastrophe nuclear – atomic issue – topic to emit – to give out
to encourage – to support to benefit – to profit negative – bad
agriculture – farming natural – organic toxic – poisonous
worried – concerned to assist – to help

8 1.g) 2.d) 3.i) 4.a) 5.h) 6.c) 7.e) 8.b) 9.f)

9 fossil fuel – *fossiler Brennstoff*
low-flush toilet – *Toilette mit geringem Wasserverbrauch*
organic farming – *biologische Landwirtschaft/ökologischer Landbau*
natural resources – *natürliche Ressourcen/Bodenschätze/Rohstoffe*
carbon dioxide – *Kohlendioxyd/*CO_2
non-profit organization – *gemeinnützige Organisation*
sustainable development – *nachhaltige Entwicklung*
nuclear waste– *Atommüll/Nuklearabfall*
global warming – *globale Erwärmung/Erderwärmung*

10 a) to be well equipped b) to explore an area (or: a region)
c) high fuel prices (or: *BE:* high petrol prices/*AE:* high gas prices)
d) water-related diseases e) high waves f) to recycle plastic
g) an important aspect h) to avoid risks i) to avoid a catastrophe
j) to donate money

11 a) Maize b) exotic c) vitamins; minerals; fibres d) Nutritious
e) calories f) rice; menu g) protein; tuna; salmon h) seeds
i) fertilisers; harvests j) pesticides; pests

Unit 7: Staying healthy in a technological world

1 embryo – embryonic defiance – defiant fertility – fertile
confusion – confused hostility – hostile behaviour – well-behaved
aggression – aggressive science – scientific confidence – confident
respect – respectful consciousness – conscious tension – tense
disappointment – disappointed anxiety – anxious

2 a) shocked (or: upset, frightened) b) emotional c) sceptical d) hesitant
e) polite (or: well-behaved) f) resentful g) hostile h) frightened
i) upset

3 reaction – to react protest – to protest fear – to fear behaviour – to behave
respect – to respect modification – to modify shock – to shock
belief – to believe

4 a) scientists; cloning b) embryonic c) duplicate d) biotechnology
e) human; human beings f) laboratory

5 a) bioengineering b) biomedical c) genetic d) Genetically modified

6 a) marrow b) organ c) liver d) stomach e) vomit f) genes
g) dehydrated h) breath i) brain j) Physical k) synthetic
l) In-vitro fertilisation; birth

7 religion – religious Jew – Jewish Muslim – Muslim Koran – Koranic
equality – equal ethics – ethical freedom – free tolerance – tolerant
virtue – virtuous

8 1.e) 2.g) 3.m) 4.h) 5.i) 6.d) 7.f)

Unit 8: Time-out

1 a) survivor b) tourist c) traveller d) hiker e) adventurer f) guide

2 a) volcano b) untouched c) accessible d) peaceful e) to depart f) bin
g) infrastructure h) forest i) barrier reef j) alive k) booking

3 a) regions b) hired; travelled c) attractions d) thunderstorm e) hurricane

4 (1) travel – *reisen* (2) catalogues – *Kataloge* (3) destination – *Reiseziel*
(4) attractive – *attraktiv* (5) faraway – *weit entfernt* (6) overnight – *über Nacht*
(7) resort – *Ferienort* (8) sporting – *Sport-* (9) sightseeing – *Besichtigung*
(10) fascinating – *faszinierend*

5 a) naturalist (the only person) b) airline (not a place)
c) sightseeing (not an adjective) d) insect (not part of a plant)
e) faraway (not a noun) f) worm (not an adjective)

6 a) Bioreserves b) Springs; thermal c) preserve d) carbon footprint
e) affect f) extraction g) survival

7 corruption – *Korruption, Bestechlichkeit;* corrupt – *korrupt, bestechlich*
economy – *Wirtschaft;* economic – *wirtschaftlich, Wirtschafts-*
budget – *Haushalt, Etat;* budgetary – *Etat-, Budget-, etatmäßig, haushaltsmäßig*
bankruptcy – *Bankrott, Pleite;* bankrupt – *bankrott, pleite*
industry – *Industrie;* industrial – *industriell*

retailing – Einzelhandel (or: retailer – *Einzelhändler*); retail – *Einzelhandels-*
wholesaler – *Großhändler, Großhandel;* wholesale – *Großhandels-*
inflation – *Inflation, Geldentwertung;* inflationary – *inflationär*

8 1.i) 2.e) 3.a) 4.j) 5.h) 6.b) 7.l) 8.k) 9.g) 10.d) 11.f) 12.c)

9

G	O	Z	V	E	L	G	N	I	I	K	S	T	E	J	S	C	I	S	N
N	R	F	U	X	O	R	C	W	L	V	A	S	G	E	W	P	Y	E	L
I	B	L	M	O	T	O	R	B	O	A	T	N	R	B	U	N	H	T	H
L	Y	O	N	B	I	B	U	L	C	H	T	L	A	E	H	X	W	A	I
C	L	A	A	E	R	O	B	I	C	S	Y	X	O	R	G	V	U	L	K
Y	W	T	G	N	I	C	N	A	D	M	O	O	R	L	L	A	B	I	I
C	U	N	Y	E	K	C	O	H	E	C	I	V	N	I	H	F	Z	P	N
P	A	R	A	G	L	I	D	I	N	G	R	U	B	X	O	C	Y	L	G

Across: jet-skiing motorboat health club aerobics ballroom dancing icehockey paragliding
Down: cycling float Pilates hiking

Unit 9: The world is getting smaller

1 trader – to trade standard – to standardize risk – to risk mixture – to mix
manufacturing – to manufacture elimination – to eliminate
globalisation – to globalise
origin – original logistics – logistical authenticity – authentic
diversity – diverse race – racial foreigner – foreign option – optional

2 standard: b) logistics: c) native: a) manufacturing: c) diversity: b)
elimination: a)

3 Suggested answers:
a) A merchant is a person who trades products in large amounts.
b) A foreigner is a person who comes from another country.
c) A trader is a person who buys and sells products.

4 Europe – European Africa – African North America – North American
South America – South American Asia – Asian Australia – Australian

5 a) globalisation; developing; chances b) manufacturing; making money
c) logistics d) ethnic; diversity e) multicultural mixture
f) global; risk; industrialized g) foreigners h) trade; guidelines

Unit 10: International politics

1 to represent – to stand for to carry out – to complete to flee – to escape
zone – area to implement – to fulfil aid – help ally – partner
to function – to work operation – action standard – criterion
committee – council to permit – to allow

2 hostile ↔ friendly majority ↔ minority direct ↔ indirect veto ↔ approval
supporter ↔ opponent stable ↔ unstable long-term ↔ short-term
constitutional ↔ unconstitutional

3 Suggested answers:
a) A commissioner is a person who acts officially for his or her government.
b) A commander-in-chief is the top leader of the military.
c) A countryman is someone who comes from your country.

4 register – *Liste, Register, Verzeichnis;* to register – *(sich) registrieren, einschreiben, anmelden* delegate – *Delegierte(r), Abgeordnete(r), Bevollmächtigte(r);*
to delegate – *beauftragen, delegieren, bevollmächtigen*
limit – *Grenze;* to limit – *begrenzen* function – *Funktion;* to function – *funktionieren*
aid – *Hilfe;* to aid – *helfen* escape – *Flucht, Entkommen, Ausweg;*
to escape – *flüchten (vor)*

5 legislation – *Legislative, Gesetzgebung;* legislative – *gesetzgebend*
judiciary – *Judikative, Justizgewalt, Gerichtswesen;* judicial – *rechtsprechend, gerichtlich*
federation – *Föderation, Bundesstaat;* federal – *Bundes-*
bureaucracy – *Bürokratie;* bureaucratic – *bürokratisch*
tragedy – *Tragödie;* tragic – *tragisch*

6 a) passes b) break c) reverse d) approve e) nominate f) afford
g) arrange

7 delegate: b) to persecute: c) illiterate: b) despair: a) hostility: a)

8 1.f) 2.a) 3.d) 4.c) 5.b) 6.e)

9 a) prevent; declarations b) humanitarian c) conditions; slums
d) migrated; persecution e) refuge f) rations

10 peacekeeping mission – *Friedensmission* desperate situation – *verzweifelte Lage*
armed forces – *Militär, Streitkräfte* refugee camp – *Flüchtlingslager*
non-governmental organization – *Nichtregierungsorganisation*
personal belongings – *persönliche Habe* safety zone – *Sicherheitszone*
short-term measures – *kurzfristige Maßnahmen*

11 **Across:** 4 orientate 5 disappear 10 concentration 12 treaty
13 executive 14 committee
Down: 1 constitution 2 democracy 3 referendum 6 accession
7 appointment 8 voter 9 bill 11 enlargement

Units 11–14: Cross-cultural communication

1 draft – to draft attachment – to attach reference – to refer (to)
appreciation – to appreciate reduction – to reduce
accommodation – to accommodate identification – to identify
response – to respond apology – to apologize inquiry – to inquire
queue – to queue confirmation – to confirm caller – to call
recommendation – to recommend request – to request
identification – to identify

2 a) appreciate b) attach c) draft d) request e) apologize f) identify
g) reduce h) call

3 inconvenience – inconvenient ethnicity – ethnic culture – cultural
uniqueness – unique intensity – intense informality – informal

4 a) informal b) unique c) inconvenience d) intense e) cultural

5 a) Pleased/Nice to meet you. b) To make a long story short, …
c) Sorry for the inconvenience. d) We'll be in touch.
e) Sorry, I didn't quite catch that. f) All the lines are busy at the moment.

6 a) maintain b) face-to-face c) dialogues d) incoming

7 1 salutation 2 reference 3 complimentary close 4 thank 5 delighted
6 brackets 7 sincerely Solution: letters = *1. Briefe, 2. Buchstaben*

8 1.e) 2.b) 3.f) 4.d) 5.c) 6.a)

9 a) cosmopolitan; overseas b) Inter-racial c) relations d) dress code
e) shake f) identifiable g) colloquial; conversations; informal
h) intense; strangers

Units 1–20: Social topics

1 a) physiotherapist b) childminder c) teacher (or: child carer) d) nutritionist
e) probation assistant f) addictions counsellor g) social worker h) warden

2 Suggested answers:
a) A nanny is a person who takes care of a family's children (at their home).
b) A teaching assistant is a person who supports teachers and pupils.
c) An official is a person who works for the state.
d) A family doctor is a doctor that families go to when they are sick.

3 supervision – supervisor – to supervise care – carer – to care
communication – communicator – to communicate judgement – judge – to judge
offence – offender – to offend terror – terrorist – to terrorize
bullying – bully – to bully

4 **Across:** → multiple sclerosis → infection ← cholera → addiction
← arthritis ← depression ← hearing loss
Down: ↓ injury ↓ blindness ↑ dementia ↑ deafness ↑ diabetes

5 a) joint; wheelchair b) bacteria c) overweight d) sign language
e) deaf; hard of hearing f) widespread; suffering

6 a) patient-centred healthcare; treatment; new-born b) radiologist; specialist; X-rays
c) maternity ward d) specialized gynecology clinics
e) Geriatric; care; patients; homes f) Accident & Emergency unit

7 **Across:** 1 bandage 4 insulin 7 antibiotic 10 donor 13 injection
14 pill 15 immune 16 surgery 17 psychology 19 mechanical heart
Down: 2 drugstore 3 outpatients 5 recovery 6 transplant 8 operate
9 check-up 11 diagnosis 12 vaccine 18 cure

8 transplant – to transplant chase – to chase donation – to donate
divide/division – to divide X-ray – to X-ray
discrimination – to discriminate (against) diagnosis – to diagnose
migration – to migrate bandage – to bandage benefit – to benefit
investigation – to investigate abuse – to abuse
medicine – medical security – secure bacteria – bacterial racism – racist
surgery – surgical deprivation – deprived society – social
illiteracy – illiterate prejudice – prejudiced excess – excessive
convention – conventional homelessness – homeless

9 1E 2G 3A 4I 5H 6D 7F 8C 9B

10 a) binge drinking; societies b) crime c) environments d) Derelict
e) welfare f) hang; cope; situation g) Drug; gang h) shoplifting
i) reprimand; guilty j) fault; punishment

11 a) victim b) settlement c) client d) self-defence e) dispute
f) quarrel (or: confrontation) g) conviction h) abuse

12 horrible – terrible severe – strict (or: serious) conventional – normal (or: typical)
disability – handicap disease – illness to cope with – to manage
operation – surgery hospital – clinic ward – unit injured – hurt

13 a) to defend (not done by an authority) b) hate (the only noun)
c) slap (not a weapon) d) terrorist (the only person) e) defence (no aggression)

14 a) occupational therapy for the elderly b) qualified childcare c) local authorities
d) drunken teenagers e) social reintegration f) social conventions
g) to commit a crime h) to give chase to a criminal (or: to chase a criminal)
i) to deny a crime j) at risk of death k) to front up a bully (or: to confront a bully)
l) social divide

Service im Internet

Unter den unten stehenden Freeway Online-Links finden Sie die Vokabeln des Vocabulary Notebook zum Download im MP3-Format, damit Sie die Aussprache hören und üben können.

Außerdem haben Sie die Möglichkeit, unter **800037-0040** die berufsspezifischen Vokabeln zu den Bereichen Wirtschaft, Technik und Sozialwesen sowie unter **800037-0030** den alphabetischen Wortschatz zum Schülerbuch einschließlich des Grundwortschatzes abzurufen.

Gehen Sie einfach auf **www.klett.de** und geben Sie in das Suchfeld den **Online-Link** ein. Der passende Link findet sich immer auf der ersten Seite einer Unit.

Unit	**Online-Link**
Unit 1	800037-0001
Unit 2	800037-0002
Unit 3	800037-0003
Unit 4	800037-0004
Unit 5	800037-0005
Unit 6	800037-0006
Unit 7	800037-0007
Unit 8	800037-0008
Unit 9	800037-0009
Unit 10	800037-0010
Units 11–14	800037-0011
Units 1–20 Social topics	800037-0015

Weitere Angebote	**Online-Link**
berufsspezifische Vokabeln zu den Bereichen Wirtschaft, Technik und Sozialwesen	800037-0040
alphabetischer Wortschatz aus dem Schülerbuch einschließlich Grundwortschatz (Deutsch – Englisch)	800037-0030